Why Do Americans Hate Americans?

A Personal Perspective on Racism in the United States of America

Written by:

Dr. Daniel Williams Jr.

BK
ROYSTON
Publishing

BK Royston Publishing
P. O. Box 4321
Jeffersonville, IN 47131
502-802-5385
http://www.bkroystonpublishing.com
bkroystonpublishing@gmail.com

Cover Design: Elite Book Covers

Photography for Front and Back Cover: Pete Stenberg

ISBN-13: 978-1-951941-80-2

LCCN: 2021900321

Printed in the United States of America

Something to Think About…

The world is not fair, so don't expect it to be fair to you. But, be fair to yourself and others, fairness will come to you.

Dr. Daniel Williams Jr.

If man cannot give life, he does not have a right to take life. This includes murder, wars, capital punishment and abortions.

Dr. Daniel Williams Jr.

Life teaches you about life.

Dr. Daniel Williams Jr.

Life is short, and time is precious.

Dr. Daniel Williams Jr.

Desperate times make desperate people do desperate things.

Dr. Daniel Williams Jr.

The two biggest problems we have in this world are fear and greed. What man cannot control, he tries to destroy. Enough is never enough.

Dr. Daniel Williams Jr.

Unresolved issues from the past affect the present and future.

Dr. Daniel Williams Jr.

History is good for history, but not necessarily for the human race.

Dr. Daniel Williams Jr.

Everyone has a story to tell, but the story is best told by its original author.

Dr. Daniel Williams Jr.

Your best years may be behind you, but your golden years are ahead of you.

Dr. Daniel Williams Jr.

Death and dying are part of life. Everyone wants to go to Heaven, but no one wants to die to get there.

Dr. Daniel Williams Jr.

Man is so brilliant, yet he is so self-destructive.

Dr. Daniel Williams Jr.

TABLE OF CONTENTS

Something to Think About

Introduction

Preface

INTRODUCTION

For quite some time, I have been contemplating writing a book. However, getting started was my biggest challenge. I have heard of "writer's block." Obviously, that could not be the case with me, because I have never written a book or believe I have what it takes to write a book. I do not believe I ever had a problem starting a project or a new venture until I had the notion of writing this book. Nevertheless, I am going to give it a shot and see what happens!

This book is based on my own personal opinions, experiences and perspectives about Americans hating Americans. Moreover, my personal perspective of racism in America will be the main focus of this book.

While the word hate is a harsh word to use, I believe it is fitting for the situation.

Not only will I discuss Americans hating Americans, I will also provide some suggestions at the end of this book, offering ways, ideas, recommendations to help Americans deal with hatred among themselves!

Even though there will be a great deal about racism discussed in this book, there will also be some discussions regarding black-on-black crime and other issues related to African Americans.

PREFACE

As stated, the title of this book is *Why Do Americans Hate Americans?* I know this title will rattle a lot of cages, because people in general do not believe they have a spirit of hate or hatred. The word *hate* is a verb, and the word *hatred* is a noun. Hate is usually in the form of an activity or attitude, and hatred can be a perception, i.e., toward a certain group of people.

My purpose of writing this book and choosing this topic is to encourage our society to address this *social disease* and work toward finding a solution. Moreover, my intention is to provide American people something practical and meaningful to use in their lives.

It is my belief that hate is predicated on *racism*, which I believe is a *social disease*. Admittedly, there are different definitions of *racism*. Regardless, *racism* is primarily based on economics, oppression and race. For instance, there was a class-action lawsuit filed against a major restaurant chain by the federal government years ago. Reportedly, this restaurant chain had some illegal practices of serving African American customers and not hiring them as restaurant managers or corporate personnel.

When an organization or person has economic power to oppress a certain race of people, based on their race, this is *racism*. I know some people tend to confuse *racism* with *prejudice* or *discrimination*. But *discrimination* is based on *prejudice*; *prejudice* is prejudging without the facts. Period.

Discrimination is choosing to *differentiate* a certain group of people based on their appearance, ethnicity, religion, customs, socioeconomic status (SES), level of education or a lack thereof, language, just to mention a few.

CHAPTER 1

Why Do Americans Hate Americans?

Why do Americans hate Americans? Actually, this is a rhetorical question, meaning that no one has a real answer to this question, and no one really knows why. Of course, we can speculate or assume, but I do not believe this question can be <u>completely</u> answered. Could it be fear? Could it be hatred? Could it be jealousy? Could it be ignorance? Or could it be just human behavior. Any one of the above can be a plausible answer, but it may not be the answer.

As America has become more diverse, people tend to misbehave. Furthermore, it seems that the more diverse we are the more divided America has become.

For instance, when a community has been predominantly one race for years and years and other people move into the community, *racism* rears its ugly head. In some cases, there is the *"white flight."* The *white flight* is a term that is often used, to describe non-minorities leaving their community when African Americans move in. When this group of people move out of the neighborhood, property value depreciates, businesses move out, redlining starts, services decline and hate crime increases, as well as poverty occurs.

I can recall when my family and I moved into a predominantly Italian American community on the far South Side of Chicago in 1969, we experienced the *white flight* syndrome. I use the word *syndrome*, because it includes characteristics related to various human behavior. For instance, some people become fearful of other people who are different from them. Some people become violent, because they feel intimidated and/or threatened. Some people may become biased and prejudiced toward minorities, because they do not understand their cultures, lifestyles, customs, clothes, music, languages, etc. Some people just do not like people who are different from themselves. Period.

Schools used to be a haven for children in America. We did not have so much violence in schools as we see today. Children would be able to attend school without being concerned about being injured and/or killed. Now, schools across our nation are rampant with school violence and/or school shootings. I can recall the very first time I personally experienced and witnessed school violence. I was in the eighth grade, returning from lunch and waiting to be allowed inside the school building. (The grade school I attended at the time was located in the "Disciples territory," but predominantly "Black Stone Rangers" attended the school). This school was totally hell! Every day I would have to fight gang members from both sides, in order to attend school and leave to go home from school.

This one particular day was quite unusual: While I and other students were waiting to be let in the school building, returning from lunch, some of the students were shouting out gang slogans when they recognized their rival gang was walking by, not driving by. The rival gang members opened fire on us. I heard bullets ricocheting off the school building, inches over my head. The Chicago police officer, who was assigned to provide safety and security to my school (James Wadsworth Elementary), returned gunfire. I could not believe what my ears were hearing. I was just a few feet from the officer as he exchanged gunfire with the Disciple gang members. This was not the only time that someone shot at me. In my junior year in high school, I was leaving for home after a fight broke out at a house party. As I was walking toward 103rd and Michigan, I heard the same familiar sounds of bullets ricocheting off the building. Immediately, I ran for cover, looking back to make sure I was not being followed or chased. What was so intriguing about this incident was that I came face-to-face with the shooter months later. Interestingly, he admitted shooting at me, but he thought I was someone else. He apologized and asked if I was hit by his gunshots, and I said, "no." This conversation took place on a CTA bus on 111th and Wallace, while my buddy and I were going home from basketball practice. Mysteriously, I felt somewhat embarrassed, because other people on the bus, including my buddy, were listening to the conversation. So, I quickly ended the conversation, stating that I was OK. My buddy never asked about the details of the conversation with this gang member. As the gang member was exiting the bus, he nodded at me, as if he seemed to be concerned. (Ironically, this same gang member once tried to recruit me when I first moved into the neighborhood). I was just a freshman in high school, attending a house party. House parties were very popular, when I was in high school. I tried to attend them as often as I could. But I stopped attending them, after the shooting incident. Instead, I decided to attend parties downtown Chicago. They were usually sponsored by adults and safer to attend. Of course, I would had to pay to get in these parties.

Do you remember me stating that I would talk about *black-on-black crime* earlier in this book? Well, I just gave you a prelude, and there is more to come. *Black-on-black crime* is just as a serious problem as *racism* in America. According to the research I have reviewed, African Americans commit crime approximately 70% against each other compared to non-African Americans committing crime against African

Americans. I have been victimized by *black-on-black crime* numerous times in my life, as well as some of my family members. A few years ago, I had a cousin who was shot to death in a black community where he lived. As of today, the perpetrator(s) has not been apprehended. To my knowledge, he was not involved in a gang or drugs. He just completed graduate school and was newly hired by the Chicago Public Schools. Both parents were professionals, so he did not fit the typical profile of a gang member or a drug dealer living in the "hood," yet he was a victim of *black-on-black crime*. When I used to live in the Woodlawn area on the South Side of Chicago, there were constant sounds of gunshots and sirens throughout the day and night. I used to fight to get in and out of the house, because of gangs. Even prior to living in the Woodlawn community, my family lived in the Washington Park community on the South Side of Chicago; this neighborhood was also infested with *black-on-black crime*. There were constant gunshots and sirens heard daily. People were killed and their bodies were dumped in alleys. Black street gangs were prevalent in the neighborhood. When I would travel from one black neighborhood to another black neighborhood, I was very cognizant of the different gangs, wanting to avoid trouble and not become a victim of *black-on-black crime*.

The majority of the inner cities in America have a serious problem with *black-on-black crime*, particularly major cities such as Los Angeles, Compton, Chicago, Detroit, Philadelphia, Washington, D.C., Baltimore, the Bronx, just to name a few.

In order to <u>seriously</u> address *black-on-black crime*, it will require the involvement of <u>all</u> Americans. I know <u>some</u> Americans may feel and believe it is "their problem," i.e., it is a problem that only affects African

Americans. This is so much further from the truth. Actually, *black-on-black crime* affects everyone in America. Obviously, we do not have an antidote or resolution to fix this problem in our country, and the black communities do not have the resources or support to address this chronic problem effectively, efficiently or efficaciously. Collectively, I believe this is the only way that we can overcome the problem.

Why Do Americans Hate Americans?

Reflection

_____

_____

_____

_____

_____

_____

_____

_____

_____

_____

_____

_____

_____

_____

CHAPTER 2

The Hate Crime Law

It amazes me to hear people say, "Things are not like the way they used to be." Are you kidding me? I am not too sure about that. Then, why the *Hate Crime Law*? A law that is designed to protect Americans from Americans. Americans who have <u>criminally</u> offended other Americans because of their race, religion, disability, sexual orientation, ethnicity or gender have committed hate crimes. I do not know if such a law exists in other countries.

In 1998, three white supremacists were charged with a *hate crime* in Jasper, Texas. Reportedly, they chained, James Byrd Jr, an African American man, to the back of a pickup truck and dragged the man's body into *literally* pieces. The man's head was severed from the torso of his body, and the back of his buttock was completely skinless, nothing but tissues and bones were visible. What an evil act this was. Only an evil person(s) would do this to another human being. Because the African American male was hitchhiking, these three white men took his life. They hated African Americans. Period. The murders of Byrd and Matthew Shepard, a gay student beaten to death in Wyoming, resulted in the expansion of the 1969 federal hate crime law in 1998.

Americans who hate Americans are <u>not</u> committing a crime. It is a *hate crime* act that is criminal. I know there are laws and legislation adopted and written to protect African Americans and other minority groups. In spite of this, we continue to have incidents of *hate crime*. I believe hate crime has escalated in the last several decades. For instance, we had the Board of Education v. Brown legislation adopted in 1954. In the amid of this law being implemented, there were <u>some</u> white women standing on the steps of white schools, protesting and fighting against school integration. Some of these white mothers said that they did not want their children going to school with African American children (Actually, the "N" word was used instead of African Americans). In some cases, people were injured and/or incarcerated. When I saw documentaries about these protests across our great nation, I felt sick to the stomach. I could not believe what I was seeing and hearing. There was so much hatred displayed by <u>some</u> white Americans toward African American students.

On Sunday, September 16, 1963, in Birmingham, Alabama, the 16th Street Baptist Church was bombed by <u>some</u> white men, killing four innocent African American girls. (By the way, black churches are still being terrorized by non-African Americans). We had the riots in the '60s due to the assassination of Dr. Martin Luther King Jr. We also had the Tuskegee experiment that lasted from 1932 to 1972; that's a total of 40 years! I was in high school, when this experiment was still in progress. It is beyond my imagination to believe that such a heinous crime was "legal" during these times in which we lived. Not one person was indicted or prosecuted, yet approximately 400 to 600 African American males lost their lives. Some believed these men were intentionally injected with the syphilis disease, to see how it affects the body when untreated. This is just amazing and unbelievable!

Henrietta Lacks was an African American woman whose cervical cancer cells were used in medical research. Mrs. Lacks' cells were used in various labs after her death. Interestingly, her cells continue to reproduce. As a result of this, Mrs. Lacks' cells have contributed to medical breakthroughs, ranging from the polio vaccine to AIDS and cancer treatments. Reportedly, Russia was even involved. Millions of dollars were made from this woman's deceased body, yet her family did not receive any proceeds from these monies. In fact, the family was not able to purchase a tombstone for Mrs. Lacks.

Virtually, racial profiling is reported every day in the news. Mostly, African American males are stopped by police for "suspicious" activities. In some cases, they are wounded and/or shot and killed by white police officers. I was once profiled in Oak Brook, Illinois, where I would go to the trail and run 4 miles on a regular basis. I have been doing this for years, before this incident occurred. What's so amazing about this incident was that I was not in my vehicle at the time. I was running with another person. After the run, we decided to go into the golf clubhouse for some water.

As we walked into the clubhouse, the cashier was apparently closing out his register. The guy who was with me noticed that the cashier had a panicked expression on his face. Because of this, he announced that we were just getting some water. (I was wondering why he believed it was necessary to announce that to the cashier, because I normally had no need to do this by myself). Nevertheless, as we were heading out of the door, I noticed an Oak Brook police car in the parking lot. I thought this was odd. So we proceeded to get into my car to go home. Less than a mile from the clubhouse, the same police officer pulled me over. Interestingly, he only asked for my driver's license. After I had given him my license, I questioned him about stopping us. Apparently, he didn't like my line of questioning and became angry, stating that, "You should be glad you are not in Chicago." He gave me my license back and left. I did not receive a ticket. I was quite upset and perturbed. The next day, I called several of my friends and shared my story with them. To my surprise, the majority of them had also been profiled. I was totally surprised! These are individuals whom I never would have expected to be profiled. They all were professionals and respectful citizens. One of them was my mentor at the time. He suggested that I contact the golf clubhouse and the Oak Brook police department, which I did. I made an appointment with the clubhouse manager and the Oak Brook chief of police. (There is a lot more to this story, but I will not go into it. However, I will mention it was an eye-opener for me, because I was so delighted to receive apologies from the police chief and club manager and free golf course time for a year). Since I am not a golfer and I really do not like golf, I was unable to take an advance of the gesture.

This situation could have gone very badly. In hindsight, my attitude could have gotten me into trouble. Yes, I was extremely angry for being stopped by the police officer without probable cause, and my line of questioning could have been a bit intimidating to the police officer. If I had to do everything over again, I would have done it differently. Firstly, I would have been less angry, but courteous. Secondly, I would have said less and responded only to the police officer's questions. I would have kept my comments to myself. Thirdly, I would have taken an accurate description of the police officer. I did not realize that I had an inaccurate description of the police officer until I met with the chief of police. (This is what happens when anger is involved. You must keep your composure and slow down your breathing. I did not do this). As an African American man, you have to be extremely careful and cognizant of the situation whenever you are stopped by the police in your vehicle. This is not the time to challenge the police. By the way, the police officer who stopped me was white.

It is my understanding that the *hate law crime* applies to other protected groups, too. However, I will not be discussing these groups because of my limited knowledge about their experiences pertaining to *racism* in America. Perhaps one day I will be able to research and learn more about other protected groups in reference to their experiences with *racism* in America. However, I would like to mention something that may be relevant: I was having a conversation with a white woman about her son and his friends charged with a *hate crime* act against an Asian American man. She did not share the details with me, but she was very upset that her son was being charged with such a crime. Obviously, she knew the seriousness of this law, because she mentioned that her son could go to prison for 6 years. As she was sharing her feelings about her son's predicament, she seemed somewhat oblivious to her son's accountability or a lack thereof. I just remained quiet and listened. There were so many questions I wanted to ask, but I did not want to upset her any more than she already was. After we had departed, I could not help but pondered the conversation, as I was wondering how this woman would have responded to my questions about her son's involvement in the *hate crime* act. Also, I had questions for her: What was her parenting style like? Where was her son's father? Did the father feel the same as she did about their son charged with a *hate crime* act? Was the father a non-minority? Did the son express any remorse? Does he feel accountable and responsible for his own action? Why does he hate Asian Americans? These were questions I wanted to ask but I did not.

I am not sure whether people charged with hate crimes are aware of their hatred toward African Americans and other minority groups. Perhaps they may not believe and/or feel that they hate African Americans. Some may believe it is not about hatred. In their eyes, it may be about their prerogative, meaning they might believe they have a right not to like everyone, including African Americans. I have an issue with this. Of course, people do not have to like each other, but no one has a right to injure or harm people because of their skin color. No one has a right to hate either.

Why Do Americans Hate Americans?

<u>Reflection</u>

_____

_____

_____

_____

_____

_____

_____

_____

_____

_____

_____

_____

_____

_____

CHAPTER 3

A Perspective on Racism in America

Racism has been a pandemic in the United States of America since its existence, and probably will be a thorn in our society until the end. Of course, it is not up to me to decide when *racism* will come to an end. Americans need to decide when *racism* will be eradicated.

Based on the research I have reviewed, *racism* is primarily based on economics, oppression and race. Theoretically, I learned a lot about *racism* when I attended the University of Illinois at Chicago, majoring in social work. My concentration was administration, policy and organization, not clinical social work.

Nevertheless, it was an interesting experience studying about the social ills of America, especially *racism* and *poverty*. Unfortunately, *racism* is a silent culprit in our society. Even though it exists, no one likes to talk about or wants to address it. There is a lot of blame, which makes it difficult for African Americans and non-African Americans to discuss and address *racism* in America, civilly, collectively and collaboratively. Oftentimes non-African Americans say that things are not like the way they used to be. Besides slavery ended over 400 years ago. But African Americans would differ, stating that things are not that much better, especially when there is job and housing discrimination, redlining, gentrification, racial profiling and hate crimes. What is so interesting about *racism* in America is that our country continues to ignore this social disease, after it has permeated our land of freedom for centuries, including now. Very little progress has been made.

Racism is not always overt or obvious. In many instances, it is covert, to the extent that is disguised and hidden. However, it does have its way of rearing its ugly head----precipitating and perpetuating repulsive practices in America. It exists in our relations and relationships with each other; it exists in our schools and colleges; it exists in our neighborhoods; it exists in stores and restaurants; it exists in businesses and corporations; it exists on our jobs; and it exists in the workforce. No one can really explain why *racism* exist, but we know it does exist. Can you imagine a world without *racism*? We would be a much better world.

Personally, I have experienced *racism* firsthand. During my college years attending graduate schools, I remember when I challenged one of my professors regarding African Americans diagnosed with severe disorders such as schizophrenia, bipolar disorders (formerly known as manic depression) more often than non-African American patients. The severe diagnoses were often given by non-African American clinicians and/or practitioners. My argument was that many African Americans were misdiagnosed with severe mental disorders. Of course, I did my research to back up my story and presented it to the class. Little did I know, my grade would suffer. Apparently, I put the professor on the spot. (I suspect out of embarrassment). He claimed that he had "black friends." (By the way, I was the only African American in the class. This was normally the case in the majority of my classes throughout my graduate college years). Usually, when a non-African American claims that he or she has "black friends," I become very suspicious. Having "black friends" does not prove anything! What matters is your heart and character. Do you treat everyone the way you want to be treated? As a non-

African American, do you address unfair treatment, injustice, bigotry or discrimination, when you encounter or witness it? This is what matters!

It is not unusual for me to be followed, when I go into stores to shop. However, my mother, who was 79 years old at the time, mentioned to me that she had the same experience. When she told me this, I was appalled! I couldn't believe that someone, like my mother, would be followed in stores where she would shop. Unbelievable!

Economics determines where people live, how they live, and what they can afford. In the inner city communities and some urban areas in America, where a significant number of African Americans live, the economy is normally depressed. Usually, African Americans have the highest unemployment rate and are jobless more often than other Americans; African Americans pay more for food, gas, auto insurance compared to non-African Americans in their communities. Services in black communities, such as public schools, garbage collection, street repairs and fire and police safety and protection, are inferior to other communities. Poverty is rampant in these communities as well as *black-on-black* crime.

According to the dictionary, oppression is defined as "unjust or cruel exercise of authority or power." For instance, when certain groups of people are unjustly oppressed by an authority figure or "the powers that be," this is a form of oppression. As stated earlier, oppression is one of the tenets of *racism*. Without oppression, there is no *racism*.

Race plays an integral part in *racism*, too. Generally, African Americans are oppressed by certain organizations, authorities, groups, economically, because of their race. Now, there are two ways *racism* is exhibited ---- covertly and overtly. Covert *racism* is subtle and not necessarily obvious, whereas overt *racism* is obvious and pretty much "in your face."

In reference to marketing, TV programs and commercials, there are subtleties of *racism.* African Americans are often portrayed as servants in shows or cast in supporting roles. It is seldom that you would see an African American in a leading role, unless it is a "black" show or movie. This is also evident in commercials and ads.

Why Do Americans Hate Americans?

<u>Reflection</u>

_____

_____

_____

_____

_____

_____

_____

_____

_____

_____

_____

_____

_____

_____

CHAPTER 4

Prejudice vs. Racism

As I stated previously, <u>some people</u> tend to confuse *prejudice* with *racism*. I have heard many times <u>some people</u> claiming that a non-African American was racist, when they should be using the term *prejudiced*. In fact, the term *racism* is often used out of context and inappropriately. Instead, *prejudice* should be used to describe the behavior and/or attitude of a person. Again, *prejudice* is prejudging without the facts. Just because a person does not like you or refuses to interact with you does not mean he or she is a racist. Perhaps the person may be prejudiced, because he or she does not know you or your character. In contrast, if an authority figure or a person who is in a powerful position oppresses you from advancing in life, economically, because of your race, then he or she is a racist! For example, I will go back to the restaurant chain I mentioned previously. There were overt and covert practices of *racism* exhibited by the restaurant, oppressing African Americans from receiving proper customer services and not affording them the opportunities to be hired and/or receive promotion within the company.

Even though the word *prejudice* has a negative connotation, it does not mean that a person is malice or evil. It just may indicate that a prejudiced person is ignorant or lacks knowledge or awareness of certain people and their idiosyncrasies. For example, African Americans are often criticized about their boisterousness and passion when they discuss sensitive topics. Some non-African Americans make prejudicial remarks about the way African Americans express themselves. Interestingly, when <u>some Italian</u> <u>Americans</u> exhibit similar behavior, they are considered to be "emotional and/or passionate."

On the other hand, *racism* is evil and repulsive. A racist person has no regard for African Americans. He or she would do anything and everything to annihilate and/or persecute African Americans. There is an evil spirit about *racism*. It causes strife, injustice, hatred, and fear.

Why Do Americans Hate Americans?

<u>Reflection</u>

_____

_____

_____

_____

_____

_____

_____

_____

_____

_____

_____

_____

_____

_____

CHAPTER 5

A Perspective on Discrimination

I find it very interesting that <u>some non-African Americans</u> and <u>some African Americans</u> are so similar in so many ways, yet they despise each other. It is safe to assume that people want to have an enjoyable, happy life, filled with good health and prosperity. Right? We know that everyone wants to live the "American dream." Right? (I have been living in America over 65 years and still don't know what this means). We know that we all want to live in peace and harmony. Right? Well, if this is the case, why do we have so much discrimination, prejudice and hatred among Americans?

I would like to tell you a true story. Years ago, I was having a conversation with a co-worker regarding how some African Americans and some non-African Americans tend to mock each other's hairstyles, skin textures, looks, complexions and clothes. The co-worker, who was a white male, made a profound statement, stating that the "White people are trying to be like black people and the black people are trying to be like white people." I could not believe he said this, but he's right! We were having a down-to-earth conversation about Americans and our relations with each other. Every day and everywhere, you can see some similarities between the two groups: Without saying, you see so many African American women with straight hair or wearing wigs. Of course, there is nothing wrong with this. (Just so you know, I am not talking about biracial women or men). There are some white women with braided hair. When I was a lad, I would see some adult African American men with their hair "processed" or straightened. Of course, you see some white men and women with dark tans. I have seen African American women with colored eye lens, especially hazel. Again, there is nothing wrong with this. However, I do have a question to ask. If there is so much dislike between <u>some African Americans</u> and <u>some whites</u>, why the similarities? Why do <u>some Americans</u> want to look like each other, in spite of the dissension, strife and discourse among them? This is so fascinating!

Discrimination is not the same as prejudice, bigotry or *racism*. The essence of *discrimination* is unjust treatment based on a person's characteristics. For instance, I will use the restaurant incident I previously mentioned as an example. African American customers were required to pay in advance before they were allowed to eat. If white customers entered the restaurant while African American customers were waiting in line to be seated, the white customers were put ahead of them, seated and served. This is *discrimination*. However, in the eyes of African Americans this could be perceived as racist and/or prejudice.

I believe the term *discrimination* can be overutilized and inadvertently, interchangeably used with *racism* and prejudice. Some people have a tendency to call everything racist, when in fact there is no *racism* involved. The fact is that some non-African Americans do not like or despise some African Americans. These individuals may not like the way some African Americans express themselves or their attire and/or hairstyle. This does not make them racists, bigots or prejudiced. Some people just do not like certain people. Period. This goes both ways; there are *some* African Americans who do not like some non-African

Americans. In essence, this is natural and human behavior. Period!

Why Do Americans Hate Americans?

<u>Reflection</u>

_____

_____

_____

_____

_____

_____

_____

_____

_____

_____

_____

_____

_____

CHAPTER 6

Is Racism A Social Disease?

Based on my personal experiences and years living in America, I strongly believe *racism* is a social disease. Now, what do I mean by this? First, there are different types of diseases. There are medical diseases such as cancer, diabetes, hypertension, etc. There are mental health diseases or mental disorders such as schizophrenia, bipolar (bipolar 1 and bipolar 2), personality disorders (narcissistic, histrionic, borderline, antisocial, just to name a few). And there are social diseases such as poverty, black-on-black crime, discrimination, bigotry, hate crime and *racism*. (In fact, I believe there are hundreds of social diseases, but I will not get into that right now. That would require another book to write).   Secondly, diseases are incurable, but are treatable. Unfortunately, there are no cures for diseases. They can only be treated, with the most efficacious, effective and antidote methods. We know that most medical diseases are primarily treated with medication and some in cases with surgery. On the other hand, mental disorders are typically treated with psychotherapy, therapy and psychological testing, with the exception of severe psychopathology, e.g., major depression, schizophrenia, or bipolar. These mental disorders often require psychotropics, because of the chemical imbalance in the brain. Oftentimes, dopamine and/or serotonin are implicated. Social diseases are a different story. However, I believe they can be treated with a different mindset---- a change of heart, genuine love, patience, caring, compassion and sensitivity. In order to treat *racism* in our society, we need to have a different mindset about people in general. We need to reconsider, treating all people the same way we want to be treated. We need to have genuine love, patience and caring toward each other. In addition, we need to be compassionate and show sensitivity toward each other. Of course, it may not be easy to do all these things, but we need to try different ways and change our attitudes about *racism* in America.

Based on the research I have reviewed, there are five stages of the grief process: *denial, anger, bargaining, depression and acceptance*. Usually, when a person is experiencing an incurable disease such as cancer in his or her life, it is likely that the individual will go through these five stages, but not necessarily in the same order as listed. A person may go from *denial* to *depression* or *acceptance* to *anger*. Why am I mentioning this? Well, I strongly believe that *racism* can make individuals experience the grief process, though, without the grieving element. Since we are talking about *racism* being a social disease, the grief process would be fitting. A racist person may deny that he or she is a racist, and probably couldn't care less. This is no different from a doctor informing his or her patient that he or she has a terminal illness. In response, the patient may deny that he or she has a terminal illness or just does not care if he or she is terminally ill. A racist may believe that he or she has a right to feel the way he or she feels about African Americans, and may not see anything wrong with hating and despising African Americans. Moreover, a racist will not be grieving over the fact that he or she denies being a racist. Grieving is immaterial, but denial is relevant, as it relates to *racism*.

Anger is the core of *racism*, and *anger* is based on hatred and evil. Hence, a racist may believe that he or she has a right to be angry with African Americans, because they might make him or her feels intimidated, threatened, and/or fearful. These feelings are expressed out of anger.

Bargaining is another stage of the grief process. Normally, when a patient realizes that he or she has not been properly taking care of his or her body, he or she may want to start making concessions and promises, wanting to change his or her lifestyle in order to have a longer life. I am not too sure if a racist wants to bargain in order to justify the reason(s) to hate African Americans. It is believed that a racist would not want to bargain for his or her racist behavior. It is a way of life, nothing else. "It is what it is." Period.

Normally, a patient becomes depressed, when he or she comes to the realization that his or her future looks bleak. The patient pretty much has given up on life and starts to feel depressed and hopeless. Getting depressed is not something that I can see a racist would experience. Depression involves feelings and emotions. It is beyond me to believe that racist people have feelings and emotions toward African Americans. Besides depression is about losses, and racist people have no love loss for African Americans.

The last stage of the grief process is the *acceptance*. When a patient has succumbed to the disease, he or she pretty much accepted his or her plight, not expecting that his or her situation will change. Racist people accept their hatred toward African Americans, and they don't make it a secret. They will be racists until the day they die! Period.

As I have stated earlier, there is no cure for diseases. However, they are treatable, provided that there is a willingness to comply with the "doctor's order."

Although I have painted a grim picture of racist people; however, I believe there is hope for them, provided that they are willing to be transformed of the mind, body and spirit. People do change, and sometimes they must call upon the Creator of the universe to help them to change. People cannot change themselves.

Why Do Americans Hate Americans?

Reflection

_____

_____

_____

_____

_____

_____

_____

_____

_____

_____

_____

_____

_____

_____

CHAPTER 7

Is America the Most Racist Country in The World?

Everyone wants to live in America, but no one wants to be an American. America is a diverse country and is the home for many people from different countries and all walks of life. Every continent is represented in the United States of America. Some people have dual citizenships. Some people have become citizens of the United States and maintain their customs, rituals, traditions, etc., but refuse to embrace the American culture and its traditions. Some people refuse to learn to speak the English language, yet they remain living in this country.

I once did an informal survey, asking some of these individuals about their experiences living in America. The vast majority of them stated that they refused to give up their native country and have plans to return to their native land. Many of these individuals expressed their disappointment about how they have been treated by Americans. They also claimed that there is a lack of respect and appreciation for their own customs, language, religion, music, traditions, etc. According to these individuals, they believe America is the most racist country in the world. I strongly believe the majority of African Americans feel the same.

Personally, I believe America is the most racist country in the world. This is based on my personal experiences and contact I have had with <u>some</u> non-African Americans. Of course, some people would disagree, and I would not be surprised! As I stated earlier, no one will admit to having an evil spirit.

I once asked my father, who was 93 years old at the time I wrote this book, how he dealt with *racism* when he was reared in Alabama? (Just so you know, my father never shared his experiences with me and my siblings about his encounter with *racism* and the "Jim Crow" laws, when he was a young and "vibrant" man). According to my father, "White people were just mean. We had to walk 9 miles to school when there was a white school just a mile from my house." My father was reared on a farm, and his father, my grandfather, was born on a plantation. One of my cousins claimed that she saw welts on my grandfather's back, when he once removed his shirt to wash up. Apparently, my grandfather was beaten like other slaves on the plantation. This same cousin's brother shared with me that their father, my father's brother, once witnessed the lynching of an African American girl. My father never shared this story with me and my siblings. I presume there is a lot my father and mother never shared with me and my siblings regarding *racism* and the "Jim Crow" laws by which they were governed. I am not sure why this was the case. Perhaps it was because of old wounds they did not want to reopen. Perhaps it was bitterness and/or anger. Or perhaps they just wanted to bury the past. In light of this, it was seldom I would inquire about their experiences as it related to *racism* in America. I do recall one day after church I asked my mother how her brothers dealt with *racism* and the "Jim Crow" laws. She provided me with an interesting response: "We told them to keep their zipper up." I had no idea what she meant by this, and I did not ask for clarification. However, I pondered her words, trying to make some sense from her statement. It took me years and having conversations with other African American women, who were from my mother's era, to finally gain a clear understanding of my mother's response. In essence, the underlying issue was about sex between white women and black men. When I first learned of this, I was completely dumbfounded and somewhat naïve. For the life of me, I could not believe that the origin of *racism* is about sex between white women and black men. Unbelievable!

There have been numerous times, as well as today, I wanted to confide in someone about my thoughts, feelings, and experiences regarding *racism*, but there was no one with which I felt comfortable sharing my emotions and concerns. Unfortunately, my brother and I do not engage in such topics. However, I am quite sure he has experienced *racism* himself. And I know that he, too, was a victim *of black-on-black* crime.

I would like to go out on the limb stating that *racism* is completely, absolutely different for African American males than African American females. The reason is that African American males are more of a threat than

African American females. African American males are perceived as oversexualized, too aggressive, dangerous and "out of control." When people see a group of African American males, it makes them uncomfortable, cringe, intimidated, and frightened and scared. African Americans males can be emotional and excitable, but some people perceive them to be loud and violent! Moreover, African American males make up the majority of the penal system. Many of them are charged and incarcerated for non-violent crimes such as drug trafficking and drug use. They have the highest homicide and mortality rates compared to their counterparts. A significant number of African American males do not live beyond the age of 18. African American males are endangered species.

On September 11, 2001, aka 9/11, America was attacked by terrorists. It was a very somber time for Americans. Fear and suspicion were rampant.

Americans were in horror and despair. The climate was solemn. I can remember the day vividly. I was in the process of changing jobs. I was leaving my administrative job with the Illinois Department of Children and Family Services to start a clinical position as a forensic psychologist at Elgin Mental Health Center in Elgin, Illinois. I decided to take a brief vacation before going to my new position with the Illinois Department of Human Services. I was actually watching TV, when the attacks occurred. There was so much confusion about the attacks, as well as inconsistent reports from the media. Like many Americans, I never thought terrorists would attack us on our own soil. However, years ago, I heard that it was a matter of time before such attacks would occur in America, because of the lack of security at the airports. Unlike other industrialized countries, we did not have the military or security presence at the airports prior to

9/11. When I first visited Japan in 1987, I was completely awestruck by the military soldiers and guard dogs at Narita Airport in Japan. I could not believe I was seeing military soldiers in army fatigues with automatic weapons. I must admit that I was taken back by the entire experience at the airport.

I often wonder whether the Ku Klux Klan (KKK) taught the world how to terrorize African Americans. Historically, the KKK was notorious for terrorizing African Americans. Our women were raped, forced into free labor and separated from their families or sold to other slave masters. Our men were beaten, castrated and lynched and forced into free labor, and separated from their families, too. African Americans were not allowed to travel without passes, and they were not allowed to enjoy the same public facilities and restaurants like non-African Americans. Even African Americans who were professionals, professional singers, musicians, athletes, politicians and celebrities were not allowed to use the front entrance of hotels and restaurants. I remember when Hank Aaron broke Babe Ruth's home run record, he stated that he was not allowed to enter the front doors of hotels and restaurants with his white teammates, when he first started playing professional baseball for the Milwaukee Braves. There were crosses burned on the front yards of professional singers' homes such as the late Nat King Cole and other African American celebrities and professionals. Many churches, where African Americans attended, were terrorized; church members were beaten and lynched. When *Brown v. Board of Education* was adopted, a law that legalized school integration, African American students were terrorized and beaten when they attempted to integrate all-white schools in different parts of the United States. Even the late governor of Alabama, George Wallace, totally ignored the law, which was successfully argued by Thurgood Marshall nearly 10 years earlier. The governor stood on the steps on June 11, 1963, at the University of Alabama, attempting to prevent two African American students, Vivian Malone and James Hood, from attending the university. The U.S. Marshals were called in to enforce the law. Here you have a public official who took an oath to serve and protect, yet he is rebelling against a federal law. Interestingly, he was not the only public official who did not obey the law. There were even other public officials and law enforcement agents who completely disregarded the law; they were not arrested or indicted for breaking the law and committing a federal crime. Just amazing!

For years, African Americans were not allowed to vote. When they were allowed to vote, they encountered unbelievable resistance at the voting polls and, in some cases, their homes were burnt down, with a burning cross in the front yard. There were whites who made it impossible for African Americans to vote by requiring illegal fees and tests to be paid and passed, respectively. In some cases, the KKK would terrorize and intimidate African Americans, so that they would not vote, as well as burning crosses on their front yards and lynching them.

Why am I talking about this in my book? Well, I believe unsolved issues from the past affect the present and future. There is a lot of unfinished business from previous eras. Yes, there has been some progress, but there is a lot more we need to address and fix in America. As I mentioned earlier, this is a *thorn* in our society, and it may not ever be removed.

I believe the two biggest problems in the United States of America, as well as in the entire world, are greed and fear: enough is never enough, and what man cannot control he tries to destroy because of fear, respectfully.

The late President Franklin D. Roosevelt once stated that the only thing we should fear is fear itself. He proclaimed this statement during the Great Depression, when this country was in ruins and despair. The economy was depressed. Unemployment was off the chart. Banks were bankrupted, closing and losing their customers' life savings. People were out of work. Countless people were homeless and dying from starvation. Moreover, suicide was rampant.

Why Do Americans Hate Americans?

CHAPTER 8

Why Americans Do Not Like Talking About Racism In America?

Talking about or discussing *racism* in the United States of America is perhaps the most avoided social issue in this country, because it creates high emotions, harsh feelings, resentment, bitterness, defensiveness and anger. There is a lot of blame. Many African Americans blame *racism* on non-African Americans, and some non-African Americans do not believe it is their fault for *racism* in this country. Hence, we are at an impasse. As I stated earlier, I believe *racism* is a social disease, one that has infected our country since its existence, as well as the beginning of the creation of the universe. I do not believe people are born as racists. *Racism* can be environmental, i.e., that it can be taught and/or learned in one's environment, e.g., in one's immediate family or circle of friends. No one likes to be blamed for something for which he or she is not responsible. I do not believe blaming is going to fix the problem, neither will making people feel responsible for something that they do not have any control over. However, people who are not interested in making changes for the betterment of the United States of America pose a tremendous challenge. Of course, there are some people who want and can make a difference in our country. This is where we can start. At the end of this book, I will make some suggestions for changes. Of course, I am not confessing that I have all the answers, but it is a start for our country to improve relationships and racial relations among ourselves, making America a better place to live and rear our families or should I say make *America great again*! Of course, we know two presidents who made this statement: Ronald Reagan and Donald Trump. I have no I idea what they meant by this statement, but I do know African Americans feel excluded by this statement. Hopefully, we are all wrong. Only time will tell.

Historically, the argument has been that what happened in the past is not the responsibility of current and future generations. In response, I would say, "yes and no," because America has not made that much progress in reference to eradicating *racism*. *Racism* is evident in virtually every aspect of our society today. It exists in our schools, communities, families, neighborhoods, churches, circle of friends and on our jobs. No one can deny that *racism* exists or is an insurmountable problem in America. As I mentioned earlier, there is racial profiling, the *hate crime law*, Tuskegee experiment and the Henrietta Lacks story. These are incidents and/or events that took place after the "Jim Crow" laws, with the exception of the Tuskegee experiment. No one can argue that *racism* is not an integral part of the American culture.

Unfortunately, there is a lot of denial about *racism* in America. Some people want to believe that *racism* is not a problem in America. Some non-African Americans claim that things are much better for African Americans. Well, I don't know about this. When African Americans have the highest morality rate, I do not believe much has changed. When African Americans have the highest unemployment rate, I do not believe much has changed. When African American youth have the highest high school dropout rate, I do not believe much has changed. When African Americans have the poorest health care among Americans, I do not believe much has changed. When there are more African Americans incarcerated, I do not believe much has changed. Now we have COVID-19 (coronavirus).

Interestingly, a disproportioned African Americans have the highest cases of the coronavirus. A disproportioned African Americans have the highest cases of the death rate due to the coronavirus. And a significant number of African Americans do not have the resources to combat COVID-19. Taking all this into account, it does not seem much has changed for African Americans. For these types of living conditions to exist in the most powerful, richest country in the world, how can you say that African Americans are living better in today's society? That is absurd!

America is a country that feeds the entire world. America is a country that has the most resources than other countries in the entire world. America is the land of opportunities. Then, if all these things are true about America, why there are so many African Americans who are living in poverty? Why do African Americans have the highest unemployment rate? Why do African

Americans have the highest mortality rate? Why do African Americans have insufficient health care or a lack thereof? Why does *racism* exist in America? Something is wrong with this picture.

Why Do Americans Hate Americans?

CHAPTER 9

A Perspective on Lesbians, Gays, Bisexuals, Transgenders and Queers (LGBTQ): As it Relates to Racism

Who cares? It is your prerogative to choose your own sexual orientation. No one has a right to tell you which orientation to choose. It does not matter if you are heterosexual, homosexual, bisexual, down-low, top or bottom, in the closet, asexual, etc. Your sexual orientation is your personal business. Period. People have a right to be treated with love, respect, compassion and caring regardless. We are all Homo Sapiens. It is safe to assume that people want to be loved and give love. Unfortunately, people who identify themselves as LGBTQ have been pretty much ostracized, ridiculed and disowned. Hey! I have something to tell you: These individuals are our loved ones. They are our relatives, siblings, friends and in some cases our parents. Nevertheless, they belong to us. They are our family. They, too, are children of God.

Unfortunately, some Americans have made LGBTQ Americans feel unwelcomed, causing them to feel alone, scared, fearful, and resentful. Because of this, this has caused a wedge between the LGBTQ community and some Americans. There are some "self-righteous" individuals who believe they have a right to be negative, critical, verbally and physically abusive and racist toward the LGBTQ community. As I mentioned previously, *racism* is based on race, oppression and economics.

Oftentimes, an individual whose sexual orientation is LGBTQ encounters job and housing discrimination, hate crime, homophobia, prejudice and *racism.*

It is my understanding that the LGBTQ community is not immune to *racism*, especially African American LGBTQ individuals. Not only there is a stigma attached to African American LGBTQ people, there is immense hatred toward them, too. To be LGBTQ and African American is a double whammy! I do not believe non-African American LGBTQ people face the same level of hatred and despair as their counterparts. African American LGBTQ individuals have to deal with *racism* as well. This definitively places them on a different platform.

Typically, when an individual(s) of the LGBTQ has been attacked, injured or murdered, there is an outcry by the LGBTQ community. I believe when any American, regardless of his or her race, sexual orientation, creed, religion, we all should be involved, demanding justice for the victim(s) and punishment for the perpetrator(s). This should also be the case when

African Americans are attacked, injured or murdered by the KKK, skinheads, the Aryan nation or victimized by *hate crime acts*. Moreover, I would like to see support from *all Americans*, to help eradicate *racism*, hate crime and discrimination against the LGBTQ community. *Racism* is a social disease that needs support from the mainstream. It is obvious that this phenomenon, as other social diseases, cannot be resolved without the help of <u>all Americans</u>! Period.

The aforementioned is based on my professional and personal experiences. I, too, have family members and relatives who are LGBTQ, and I love them dearly!

Why Do Americans Hate Americans?

CHAPTER 10

Thank God for Women

Thank God for women! Without women, there would be no United States of America. Our American women kept this country running and functioning during the World War II (WW II). They provided the military with food, clothes, supplies and made ammunition, tanks, airplanes and other weaponry for the American GIs. Chicago was one of the military hubs during WW II, where the majority of the employees were women. The Chicago O'Hare Airport used to be the location where the military plant was located.

Women kept this country afloat during WW II. They were the pillars of our communities and the backbone of our country. If they were not proficient, tenacious, smart, efficient, determined and focused, Germany probably would have won the war, and America would not be the country it is now!

Have you ever heard that "for every good man there is a good woman behind him?" The woman is his mother. She is the one who trains, shapes, molds and prepares him for the future. I have gotten into many arguments with married women who believe they are the women who shaped, molded and prepared their husbands. In other words, many of them believe they are the ones who should receive credit for their husbands' character, success, etc. Perhaps some women may have contributed to their husbands' success, but I do not believe they are responsible for preparing their husbands to become the men they have become. I once had a conversation with a woman who was a mother, grandmother and great grandmother about this topic. She is the one who told me that the mother, not the wife, who develops, rears and shapes her son to become the man he has become. I must agree with her. My mother receives the credit and "criticism" for whom I have become.

Now, what is my point here? Why am I saying this? Well, it saddens me to hear the media reporting women are not receiving the credit and respect they deserve. There have been reports of unequal pay for equal work. On the average, women's income is less than men's income. There are, significantly, fewer women who are presidents of corporations, businesses, banks, etc. There are fewer women who are entrepreneurs. There are more single women who are the head of their households.

For the past several decades, there have been women's groups protesting against discrimination and unfair labor that many women have experienced. I would be remiss, if I did not acknowledge the validity of these claims. However, there is much more to these claims that meets the eye. Firstly, I strongly believe women have a tremendous amount of power and influence. Secondly, I strongly believe women can make a difference in our society. (Actually, women have made a difference in our society, and I strongly believe they will continue to make differences, becoming trailblazers and leaders in all aspects of our nation). Thirdly, I strongly believe women are in control of their own density. Finally, if women were to represent and celebrate all women from all races, they would be more powerful than men and definitely receive the credit they deserve. Representing and celebrating women from all races, ethnicities and socioeconomic classes is the biggest obstacle women face.

Many women believe this is a "man's world." Well, this is not so. This is a *white* man's world, and I do not mean this in a disrespectful way. Whenever I hear women make such an untrue statement, it makes me cringe. I cannot believe that there are so many women who believe this, when they know for a fact that African American men have the highest unemployment rate, the highest incarceration rate, the highest high school drop-out rate and the highest mortality rate. There is no way African American men are among this privileged group. Please, do not say this is a man's world. This is a *white* man's world. Period.

It is very difficult for me not to believe that some women do not realize their authoritarian position in our society. Women play an integral role in our society. They pretty much run our families, rear our children, support their husbands in their pursuits and are, in some cases, the breadwinners in their families, particularly in the majority of African American families.

The progress for women has been proliferating for the past few decades. For instance, there are more women in politics as state governors, legislators, mayors, etc. There are more women in the workforce than men. More women are presidents of companies and businesses and chief executive officers (CEOs) in the media compared to several decades ago. Some of the richest people in the world are women. I strongly believe within the next 10 years, America will have its first female president.

So, why is there so much noise from women's groups about women are not receiving their fair share? I know many African American women do not feel they are getting their fair share and believe that they are not represented and celebrated by other women.

African American women have been at the bottom of the totem pole since they were first brought from Africa. They took care of their families and their slave owners' families. Many of their slave owners raped and impregnated them, to have biracial children. They were beaten and lynched. (One of my uncles witnessed a black female lynched, when he was a child. I could not believe black women were lynched. When I first heard about this, I was in disbelief). African Americans women have fought fearlessly and endlessly to have their children educated prior to and during the *Brown v. Board of Education* era. During this time period, I watched many documentaries showing white women who were fighting vehemently, viciously and ferociously against school integration. I was totally appalled and saddened, watching these documentaries.

I once watched a documentary pertaining to three women: One was a Jewish mother, a Muslim mother and a Roman Catholic mother. In the documentary, they all were asked about their preferences and wishes for their children in reference to marriage. Surprisingly, they all stated that they wished their children <u>not</u> marry outside their ethnic group, meaning Jews should marry Jews, Muslims should marry Muslims and Roman Catholics should marry Roman Catholics, yet they all wanted world peace and harmony. I could not believe what I was hearing from these three mothers. I thought how would we ever have world peace and harmony, when interracial marriages are prohibited? In general, people want to marry the person with whom they have fallen in love, not because of someone's ethnic background, race or religion. My mother once told me that "You cannot control falling in love with another person." When she first told me this, I disagreed with her. At one time, I believed people have the control to fall in love with whomever they please. Boy, I was wrong! It took me a few years to appreciate what my mother was telling me about falling in love and being in love. They are completely different spheres in the makeup of humans. Falling in love and being is love is not synonymous.

Historically, it was illegal in the United States of America for an African American to date or marry a white person. If I am not mistaken, there are still some states that prohibit interracial dating and marriage. Even though these laws still exist in some states in America; however, they are not enforced. Interestingly, during slavery some slave owners procreated a new race, "mulatto." Reportedly, mulattos were only allowed to marry other mulattos. There were some cases where mulattos would be able to pass for white and live in only white neighborhoods.

It is my belief that when people are not allowed or prohibited to marry outside their races, this can create resentment and animosity. Because of this, people may feel that they are not "good enough" to marry someone who is not from the same race or ethnic group, causing people to have ill feelings and a misconception that they are inferior. Of course, this does not help *racism* in America. Marriage is supposed to be about love! Period.

Why Do Americans Hate Americans?

CHAPTER 11

What Does Fear Have to Do with Racism in America?

Fear is a motivating factor in virtually everything we do in life. For instance, the stock market is affected by consumers' and buyers' level of confidence. If they do not have confidence in the stock market, it will likely not do well. As a result, this will have an adverse effect on the market, as well as on our economy. If people are fearful of taking vacations to a certain part of the world due to fear, they will not travel to that country. If the country depends on tourism for financial support for its economy, the country might go into a recession. Salespeople often utilize fear as a strategic method to entice people to buy their products and goods and services. For example, when you buy an expensive electronic device such as a flat screen TV or a cell phone, the salesperson often pushes an extended warranty, implying that you may need it, because the product may not last. Of course, you will feel compelled to purchase the warranty out of fear, not wanting to be with an expensive electronic device that no longer works and you do not have no warranty for the defected product. During the Great Depression era, some people were fearful and devastated after losing their life savings and committed suicide. When some people are fearful of other people for various reasons, they have a tendency to become aggressive, hostile and/or violent. This has been the case between some non-African Americans and African Americans. Hence, fear can be the underlying issue of *racism*. As stated earlier, African Americans are treated badly because of fear. Some non-African Americans are extremely fearful of

African Americans. Because of this, *racism* arises and animosity, hatred and resentment occur.

Why Do Americans Hate Americans?

Reflection

_____

_____

_____

_____

_____

_____

_____

_____

_____

_____

_____

_____

_____

CHAPTER 12

The COVID-19 Pandemic (Coronavirus): As it Relates to Racism

During the writing of this book, the *COVID-19* pandemic (coronavirus) has invaded the entire world. All the continents have been affected by it, and there is nothing but fear, panic and uncertainty on the minds of the people. While the world leaders are trying desperately to get a grasp on this calamity, some people are not taking this deadly virus seriously. Yet, people around the world are dying by the droves, including Americans.

Reportedly, the *COVID-19* was first discovered in Wuhan, China, in 2019. However, there have been reports that this virus was predicted approximately 10 to15 years ago. The validity of this might be a bit challenging to prove. Nevertheless, the *COVID-19* is suspected to be a "man-made" virus. If this is true, it is so unfortunate and sad.

The origin of the *COVID-19* is from a non-Christian country, China. China is predominantly a Buddhist country with a population of approximately 1.4 billion people. The timing of the coronavirus comes at a very interesting time: While the virus was detected in China at the end of 2019, it emerged in the United States of America during the Lent season, one of the important, if not the most important, Christian holidays in America. Even Christians who do not attend church on a regular basis are likely to attend church and celebrate Easter. Easter is also a time when families, relatives and friends break bread together. Parents buy their children special clothes for Easter, as well as Easter candies, eggs to color and coloring books.

What I am about to share with you is based on my own personal speculation and suspicion. Before I start discussing the *COVID-19* pandemic, I would like to provide some historical background about some of the viruses we have had in America, starting with the smallpox virus. Reportedly, the smallpox virus was engineered by a British officer and planted on blankets that were given to the Native Americans. Consequently, the Native American population was annihilated. Since then, the Native Americans have not been able to recoup from this heinous, evil act. Now, this is a race that seems to be slowly dying and disappearing from the human race. I hope that this will never happen. By the way, my paternal grandmother is Black Foot and my paternal grandfather was born on a plantation.

During the 1980s and 1990s, the Acquired Immune Deficiency Syndrome (AIDS) virus surfaced in

America. Reportedly, AIDS was also a "man-made" virus manufactured by some German Nazi scientists in the 1930s. Reportedly, the virus was injected in humans. Initially, the media were reporting that this was a "gay disease," claiming that gays were the only ones who were affected by AIDS. Of course, we know this was not the case. However, the damage was already done. The gay community was ridiculed, ostracized and attacked viciously. Many gays who were afflicted with AIDS were illegally discharged from their jobs, leaving them without health insurance and medical services. There was so much misinformation and bias toward the gay community. When the mainstream was also affected by AIDS, everything changed. It was no longer a "gay disease." Gays were not the only ones who were afflicted by AIDS. In fact, some professional athletes and celebrities were diagnosed with AIDS, as well as thousands of people from the general population.

Another controversial virus was syphilis. Reportedly, the syphilis virus was injected into the bodies of poor black sharecroppers. This was also known as the *Tuskegee experiment.* The onset of this experiment started in 1932 until 1972. We know that this virus was intentional and illegal. There is no doubt how and why the *Tuskegee experiment* was implemented. Basically, it was an experiment to determine the effect of the syphilis had on the human body when gone untreated. Approximately, 4,000 to 5,500 black males lost their lives, and many of their wives and children were affected by the experiment, too.

There have been other viruses, such as Ebola, SARS, and anthrax, that have impacted America, but nothing like *COVID-19*. This virus is like a vacuum cleaner, sucking up lives at an extremely rapid speed in a very short period of time. At this time, there is no cure, vaccine or medicine that can fight off this deadly virus.

I am having a very difficult time believing that the aforementioned viruses are "man- made." I guess I should not be that surprised knowing the history of man and his malevolent behavior. I often say that man is so brilliant, yet he is so self-destructive! Greed and fear are the two biggest culprits for man. Enough is never enough, and what man cannot control, he tries to destroy out of fear.

While the leaders of the world are trying to find ways, methods and a vaccine to fight off the *COVID-19*, as well as keeping us safe and alive, there are so many Americans who are anxious to get back to "business as usual and normalcy." Americans are constantly warned about this deadly virus, yet many of them are not taking this virus seriously. A majority of the states of America have issued a stay-at-home order, but there are still a few others that have not followed suit. In fact, there are some restaurants continue to stay open to the public, and people are dining in these restaurants. Unbelievable!

It saddens me that the guru of epidemiology and an infectious disease specialist, Dr. Anthony Fauci, who is helping the president to battle *COVID-19*, has been receiving death threats on his life. As a result, Dr. Fauci and his family members are now receiving security and protection. I cannot believe anyone with an ounce of intelligence would do such a repulsive and evil thing. Dr. Fauci is perhaps one of the few individuals who can guide us through this calamity, yet there are <u>some</u> Americans who want to harm him because they are not hearing what they want to hear from him. I had a conversation with my friend who lives in Japan about this, and he believes it is people from the *"right wing."* I disagreed. He asked me what kind of people would do this and what is on their minds. Obviously, he was implying that it must be individuals who have a mental disorder. In response, I reminded my friend that we live in an evil world, and there are evil people among us. It is not always individuals afflicted with mental illness or mental disorders who are causing harm to other people. Some people are just evil. Period!

Whenever *COVID19* gets under control, there will be changes. These changes will be essential, vital, critical, crucial and necessary. For example, the way we interact and socialize with each other will change; the way we worship in churches, synagogues, cathedrals and mosques will change; the way we educate our children and attend colleges and universities will change; the way we dine out at restaurants will change; the way companies and organizations hire and train their employees will change; the way consumers shop and buy merchandise and do business will change; the way we travel and take vacations will change; and the way we receive dental and medical care will change. The visit to the doctor's office will change, as well as going to the dentist. This virus will create a new paradigm shift in our lives, to a point where we will not recognize our previous lives after a few years. The world will behave, look and feel differently!

Interestingly, the media have reported a disproportioned African Americans who have been afflicted with *COVID-19*, as well a disparity of medical care and intervention for *COVID-19*. Hence, the majority of the victims who have died from the coronavirus are African Americans, yet African Americans only compose of approximately 12% to 13% of the population in America. Based on the research I have reviewed, African Americans tend to have poorer health than non-African Americans. African Americans tend to receive insufficient health care compared to non-African Americans. African Americans have the highest rate of heart disease than non-African Americans. African Americans have some of the highest rates of diabetes, cancer, high blood pressure than non-African Americans. This is the case in the majority of the inner cities where African Americans live.

According to Chicago Mayor Lori Lightfoot, who is also African American, this is unacceptable. She wants the medical profession to share the demographics of medical information with the African American communities across the nation so that they can share this information with African Americans, advising them of these dire numbers. The thought is that if African Americans are made aware of these numbers and provided with resources, prevention, intervention and education, they will be better informed and might make healthier changes/choices in their lives. I believe Mayor Lightfoot wants to collaborate with other inner city mayors where African Americans prevalently live so that there will be an effort to improve African Americans' health and lifestyle.

Actually, I am not surprised by all of this, because I have studied demographics related to African Americans' education, welfare, health care and infrastructure for years. What surprises me now is that this issue is attracting attention. Perhaps something will be done about this, but I am not too sure anything will happen. This is not new. Health care has always been an issue for African Americans, especially the impoverished, marginalized and disenfranchised. I really don't want to be cynical about this, but the African American community has been in need of quality health care and other necessities and sustenance for centuries. I guess we would have to wait and see, if the situation changes. I hope it will change.

As I reflect on the different kinds of viruses that have afflicted humankind, I noticed one thing that they all have in common: Allegedly, they all were manufactured by man. As stated earlier, man is so brilliant, but he is self-destructive. There is nothing that man cannot do on this earth, but his appetite for greed, as well as his obsession with fear, causes him to do more harm than good for his or her fellow brethren. Unfortunately, these viruses mostly affected African Americans, who already have the highest mortality rate in the world. African Americans are without proper health care, resources, jobs, schools and services in their communities. Having to deal with viruses such as *COVID-19* places a tremendous burden on this population. It is beyond my imagination and comprehension what could be on the minds of African Americans, enduring *COVID-19* and other iniquities.

Some people do not believe the viruses that we have endured and fought were allegedly manufactured and created by their own people. Viruses just don't come from nowhere. These are calamities that are designed to kill and destroy. I do not believe *COVID-19* is a fluke or an accident; I also do not believe the coronavirus originated from bats. This is the same myth that HIV, or human immunodeficiency virus, which causes AIDS, was originated from monkeys.

What is so intriguing about *COVID-19* is that people are behaving in peculiar ways. I have noticed people without masks and socializing fewer than 6 feet. Some people are walking side-by-side, talking very closely to each other, sneezing and laughing without a care in the world. I am also seeing groups of teenagers and families riding their bikes, definitely fewer than 6 feet.

No one is wearing a mask. Also, I see parents teaching their small children to ride tricycles, without masks. This entire situation is so interesting and extraordinarily scary!

At the onset of *COVID-19*, Americans were strongly advised to stay inside and only go out for essential things such as grocery and medication. However, a significant number of Americans have completely ignored this advice. Instead, they are behaving as if *COVID-19* does not exist.

A few weeks ago, some states began to slowly open up, with restrictions and stipulations, meaning that people follow CDC guidelines, i.e., keeping social distancing, wearing masks and sanitizing their hands frequently. Unfortunately, a significant number of Americans are not following these protocols.

Why Do Americans Hate Americans?

CHAPTER 13

My Personal Perspective on Black-on-Black Crime

Black-on-black crime is very dear to me, mainly, because I am an African American, and I have been victimized by it, as well as some of my family members. In fact, one of my cousins was killed by an African American(s).

Black-on-black crime is a serious problem in America, and it has been for quite some time. As I stated at the beginning of this book, I strongly believe that *black-on-black crime* is a social disease. Many people believe that this issue can only be resolved by African Americans themselves. I disagree. If this were the case, I would not be writing about it. This phenomenon has impacted the black communities, to the extent that no one really knows what to do about it. It is unfortunate that there has not been that much progress made to address this chronic problem in America. Even African Americans do not have an answer to *black-on-black crime*. What is so interesting about *black-on-black crime* is that it also affects non-African Americans.

As I stated, *black-on-crime* is a social disease, i.e., it is incurable but treatable. I believe if *black-on-black crime* became a major priority, we would not have this problem in America. In order for this to happen, interested groups, e.g., women's group, LGBTQ, churches, etc., would need to help directly. Getting non-African Americans involved is perhaps the only way to eradicate *black-on-black crime*. I do not believe leaving the problem up to African Americans to fix will ever happen. African Americans do not have the resources or power to resolve *black-on-black crime* in their communities. One may think African Americans should be able to fix their own problem. This is further from the truth. In light of this, there is no cause and effect involved. Just because *black-on-black crime* is predominantly in black communities does not mean that African Americans are the reasons that this problem exists, chronically. I know this for a fact, because my family and I have lived in black communities and we were not the cause of the problem.

I have a story to share with you. When my family and I used to live in the Washington Park community in the 1960s, my father would gather the neighborhood youth and take them to Washington Park to play softball on Sundays during the summer. (This occurred every year until my parents divorced). My father would give me money to go to the local record store to purchase a 16-inch softball and a case of Coke Cola for the boys. As a result of this, my father became known in the neighborhood; the boys often asked me on Sundays, if there will be a softball game. In response, I would say either, "I don't know" or "no." My "no" response was based on how I was feeling. Typically, I would not participate in the Sunday softball games, due to my jealousy and feeling neglected by my father. There were a few times my father made me attend and participate in the Sunday softball games. I must admit it was not a good experience for me. I would had preferred to have my father to myself playing with him.

My reason for sharing this story was to point out that there were other males who took the time to try to make a difference in the black community. My father was not the only African American who interacted and socialized with the youth in the neighborhood. There are still African American males who are involved in their communities. I know there are mentors and community organizations who give their time, money and effort to make a difference in black communities, but more people are desperately needed.

I strongly believe that the black communities need other people involved in fighting against the *black-on-black* crime epidemic. There are too many factors that impede on the fight against *black-on-black crime*, making it impossible for African Americans to take on this battle themselves.

Black-on-black crime is often portrayed by the media as a black people problem. The media seldom show anything positive about the black community combating *black-on-black crime.* Perhaps the media believe that *black-on-black crime* is a hopeless situation in the black community.

Why Do Americans Hate Americans?

Reflection

_____

_____

_____

_____

_____

_____

_____

_____

_____

_____

_____

_____

_____

_____

CHAPTER 14

Some People Do Not Behave Themselves

I often wonder why some people do not behave themselves, meaning do what is right and do the right thing. As I have stated earlier, *racism* is a colossal phenomenon in our society as well as in the entire world. *Racism* is about people who do not do what is right. *Racism* is about people who want to be superior to other people. *Racism* is about people who believe they are entitled to make other people to feel inferior and invaluable. In essence, *racism* is about exploitation, cruelty, fear, greed and hatred. *Racism* would not exist if people behave themselves. Perhaps some people believe they are beyond rapprochement. They may believe they do not have to follow laws and rules and regulations, like the rest of us. They may believe they are indestructible and not indispensable.

Following rules, laws and regulations may be perceived as unnecessary for some people. Some people may only do what is right to a certain extent. We have rules and laws for a purpose. Even individuals who are the most upright citizens may be challenged by doing what is right and fair consistently. We need rules, laws, and regulations to help us to maintain civility and order in our society, as well as in the world. If people are allowed to do whatever they want to do, to whomever, regardless, we will live in constant chaos and fear.

Personally, I believe it is always best to do the right thing. Period. You cannot go wrong by doing what is right. I am a strong believer of karma: You will reap what you sow. I have witnessed and experienced karma first-hand, and I know it can be <u>something</u> else.

Why people do not behave themselves is something I have always wonder about. It seems so simple and easier to treat people with kindness, respect, love and compassion. Of course, this is ideal and may be unrealistic, as well as naïve. Nevertheless, people need to be held accountable for their own action and/or behavior. There is no excuse for bad behavior. When I worked in psychiatric inpatient facilities, working with patients with mental disorders, we held our patients accountable when they would become physical and verbally aggressive. If individuals who are afflicted with mental illness are held accountable for their maladaptive behavior, it is only right and fair for individuals without mental illness to be held by the same standards. Right?

Why Do Americans Hate Americans?

<u>Reflection</u>

_____

_____

_____

_____

_____

_____

_____

_____

_____

_____

_____

_____

_____

_____

CHAPTER 15

Racial Relations between Blacks and Whites

Racial relations between blacks and whites have always been intriguing and somewhat problematic in America for centuries. Racial relations can be business matters, community and social issues, economic possibilities, job opportunities, politics, etc. Prior to COVID-19 and the protests, there have been very few racial relations between blacks and whites. Everything has been pretty much as business as usual. But now, there are blacks, whites and others who are protesting in the streets and communities across America. I have seen practically every race represented in these protests and demonstrations that are happening in America. Where have all these people been after all these years? This is not the first time we have had occurrences of African Americans beaten and killed by police officers. Why now? What will happen once things settle down?

This entire situation makes me a bit suspicious of <u>some</u> people's motives. Are they genuine and sincere about protesting and chanting for changes? Are they genuine and sincere about wanting to eradicate "*systemic racism*?" Or, is this performative activism or surface-level activism?

Blacks and whites have been at odds on a variety of issues and matters related to *racism*. This is not new. What is new is that there is a lot of noise about "Black Lives Matter." Blacks' lives have always mattered. It seems that everyone is jumping on the bandwagon about "Black Lives Matter." Black people do not need people to tell them that their lives matter. They already know this! The issue is do white people know that black people matter in America? I believe the record speaks for itself. The United States of America was built on the backs of black people. Even the White House was built by black people (or should I say slaves). Black people have been recognized for numerous inventions and contributions that benefited white people in this country. Black people have fought in every war in which this country has been involved, even when Black GIs were denied the respect and recognition that many of their fellow white GIs received. The famous Tuskegee Airmen are a perfect example of how blacks bravely and skillfully fought in World War II, but they still were subjected to discrimination within the United States military. It took years after World War II, before the Tuskegee Airmen received recognition for their valor service for America. Some of the best doctors, surgeons, lawyers, scientists, athletes, celebrities, singers, musicians, educators, politicians and police officers are black. Of course, "Black Lives Matter!" It does not take a rocket scientist to know this. Unfortunately, there is another *virus* that is causing white people not to acknowledge that "Black Lives Matter," prior to the *propaganda* we are seeing across our great country---the blame game! Black people blame white people for *racism* in America; and white people blame black people for being the victims of *racism.*

As I have stated previously, blaming white people will not fix the problem, and blaming black people for their predicament will not fix the problem, too. An action plan is needed so that racial relations between blacks and whites can improve in America. Whites and blacks need to be part of this action plan. This action plan needs to benefit <u>all Americans!</u>

Ideally, an action plan works from top-down to bottom-up. Exactly, what do I mean by this? In reference to top-down, whatever resources are already in place, we need to utilize them accordingly. For instance, laws and policies need to be implemented expeditiously, fairly, and equitably. We should not have different laws and policies for blacks who live in the inner cities and whites who live in the suburbs. Blacks and whites need to work together to make sure that there are effective and fair opportunities for employment, job advancement, job recruitment for qualified blacks and whites, not based on office politics or preferential treatment.

Regarding bottom-up, blacks and whites need to work together for a common cause, i.e., they need to work to have harmony and peace among themselves. They need to open their neighborhoods and communities and invite each other to live in and/or visit their communities. Getting to know someone who is not of your race and background is a great way to start the process.

Racial relations involve having contact and association with other people regarding business transactions, politics, economics, socialization and justice. For example, some African Americans do not believe that they would get a good deal or bargain on a brand new vehicle. I believe the majority of African Americans do not believe that they would not be treated fairly, when doing personal business with non-African Americans. Based on the research I have reviewed, the majority of African Americans believe race plays an integral part in business transactions. According to credit reports, a significant number of African Americans do not have good credit scores, which places them at risk of higher interest rates and paying more for merchandise, good and services than their counterparts. Moreover, African Americans have a very difficult time securing mortgage loans and small business loans compared to non-African Americans. Some people may believe that African Americans do not know how to manage their money, which may cause them to be denied for loans and credit. In light of this, African Americans' income tend to be significantly less than their counterparts, placing them in a lower socioeconomic status (SES) with less buying power. Now there is a flip side to this, too. I have often heard that some African Americans do not like dealing with other African Americans when money and business are involved. This includes not supporting and patronizing black-owned businesses. This may seem odd, and it is. African Americans not supporting African Americans is not something new. Unfortunately, there is no clear explanation why this is the case. Some may believe that black business people or black entrepreneurs are not business-minded, meaning that they are not professional, efficient, proficient or effective. Of course, this is not true. There are some excellent African Americans entrepreneurs. The stigmatization of African Americans may have a negative impact. Because of this stigma, many black businesses suffer and do not survive in the business world. African Americans whose credit history is spotless can be affected by this, too. Because of their race and ethnicity, they are less likely to be approved for credit and/or loans for businesses and mortgage loans. Some people call this *institutional racism. Institutional racism* is implicated in matters related to African Americans regarding education, ownership of businesses, property, employment, politics, health care, social issues, justice, etc. For example, one of the reasons that so many inner city public schools have poor education and few resources is because of the majority of the students are African Americans and Hispanics. Here in

Chicago the public schools (CPS) in the inner city are deplorable. School buildings are dilapidated; school books are outdated and tattered; teachers are overwhelmed by the large classroom sizes; and schools are rampant with school violence. As a result of this, African Americans students are not able to learn in safe environments that are conducive to learning.

When I was attending graduate school, I read a book about politics, economics and race pertaining to America. It was an illuminating book discussing politics in America, and the impact politics has on our economy and races. One of the main tenets I learned about this book was how certain ethnic groups and races control politics in America. According to the book, the majority of our American politicians, who control politics in America, are Irish Americans and Italian Americans. Moreover, virtually everything is predicated on politics in America. There is office politics, school politics, sports politics, church politics, medical politics, law politics, research polities, media politics, etc. There is nothing that functions or operates in America without the influence of politics. I have often heard that it is not "what you know, but who you know." Some people may get jobs or promotions, because they know someone in a powerful or political position.

Some people may get a break from a court case, because they knew someone in the court system. Some students may receive a higher grade in classes, because their parents are donors to the university or college. Some students who are applying to a certain university or college may receive preferential treatment, because their parents know the president of the university or college. Not everyone has "political connections." Usually, African Americans would need to attain jobs and promotions on their own merits. This is not always the case for non-African Americans.

I would like to talk about something that may be a bit odd, but relevant to this section of my book, and that is *dysfunctionality* in American families. When I was attending graduate school, studying for my doctorate in clinical psychology, I learned that a significant number of American families are *dysfunctional*. One of my professors claimed that over 85% of American families are *dysfunctional*. A *dysfunctional* family tends to have constant chaos and confusion in its family dynamics. Family members are not able to come to an agreement on simple things such as meal preparations, family budget or paying the bills, family vacation plans, etc. There is a lot of discord, dissension, despair and confrontation in a *dysfunctional* family, as well as domestic violence. I was reared in a *dysfunctional* family myself. Moreover, some *dysfunctional* families have generational curses in their households, i.e., family history repeats itself with the *dysfunctionality* from generation to generation, until the generational curses are broken.

The etiology of dysfunctionality in American families is complicated and complex, as well as idiopathic. Obviously, each family dynamics differs from family to family, as well as from generations from generations. In spite of this, the vicious cycle must be broken so that the dysfunctionality can be eradicated. Sometimes it may take an older person to initiate changes within his or her immediate family. For instance, I am trying to break the generational curses and dysfunctionality with my own daughters and grandchildren. I hope that they will be willing to embrace the changes and continue with them in their own immediate family dynamics.

What African American families and non-African American families have in common regrading *dysfunctionality* and generational curses is *maladaptive behavior*. *Maladaptive behavior* is abnormal behavior. For instance, we know that it is not normal for families to live in chaos and confusion. We know that it is not normal for families to hurt and injure each other; we know that it is not normal for families to live in poverty and despair; and we know that it is not normal for families to <u>hate</u> people because of their skin color, gender, sexual orientation, SES, religion, customs or beliefs.

Do you recall me stating that unresolved issues from the past affect the future and the present? Well, I like to do some historic writing for a moment.

In 1964, the Civil Rights Act was adopted and passed into law, giving African Americans a chance to live decent lives. In theory, this Act prohibited unfair treatment and practices in reference to employment, hiring practices, job opportunities, school segregation, housing, etc. for African Americans. Unfortunately, this Act was virtually *"repealed"* by the late president

Ronald Reagan. This administration thwarted any possibilities for African Americans to benefit from the Civil Rights Act, as it was intended to be executed into law. Even when Congress passed the Civil Rights Act, African Americans were not <u>completely</u> benefitting from it. There was still unfair treatment and racial discrimination in America. But, when Ronald Reagan became president, everything came to a complete halt! African Americans were suffering tremendously. Jobs and decent housing were scarce. Schools in black neighborhoods were deplorable and dilapidated and without sufficient funds and resources. Ronald Reagan stated that it is not the federal government's responsibility to educate the people. He continued to say that in order to receive a quality education, you must pay for it! This administration had no mercy on the African Americans. What little progress that was made by blacks was taken away by Ronald Reagan.

Since then it has been an uphill battle for African Americans to live in America. I believe this is one of the major unresolved issues from the past that is affecting our present and future in this country.

Why Do Americans Hate Americans?

Reflection

_____

_____

_____

_____

_____

_____

_____

_____

_____

_____

_____

_____

_____

_____

CHAPTER 16

Perceptions of African Americans

Perceptions of African Americans can vary from person-to-person. As I have mentioned previously, African Americans are not monolithic, i.e., they are not all the same. However, some non-African Americans have similar perceptions of African Americans, based on prejudice. Remember earlier, I defined prejudice as prejudging without the facts.

Years ago, I had a conversation with a very good friend who is Nigerian regarding perceptions. He and I got caught up in a dialogue about the significance of perception. His belief was that perceptions are very important, and my belief was that they were not. The dialogue ended in an impasse. As years have gone by since our conversation regarding perceptions, I have begun to have an appreciation for my friend's assertion of perceptions. Now I completely and totally agree with him. Perceptions are extraordinarily vital and essential in the American culture. Although perceptions are not based on research or empirical evidence; however, they do weigh significantly on the minds of many, if not, the majority of Americans. Specifically, the perceptions of African Americans can be elusive and biased, without any truth to it. For example, the perception of the African American male may be that he is dangerous, violent, out of control, uneducated, irresponsible, lazy, belligerent, loud and over sexualized. The perception of an African American female may be that she is over sexualized, belligerent, obnoxious, and uneducated. Moreover, the perception of an African American male is perceived as a threat to non-African Americans, whereas the African American female is not perceived as a threat to non-African Americans.

Although there is no research to support these perceptions of African Americans, some people believe them and behave accordingly. For instance, I have been in the presence of white females who have clenched their purses, as if I were going to snatch their purses. This used to bother me whenever this would happen, but not anymore. It is so sad and unfortunate that people behave this way. Now I must admit that I have had similar experiences with black women. I can recall one incident, vividly, when I was working in Oak Park, Illinois. I was walking down the street behind a black woman. Suddenly, she turned around, clinching her purse, and charged at me, as if she were a running back. I could not believe what I was seeing. I yelled at the woman and asked what she was doing? She did not respond and continued to rush by me. She almost knocked me down. Unbelievable!

I have been told many times that I am intimidating and too tall. Both non-African Americans and African Americans have told me this. I do not know why some people perceive me to be intimidating. I do not believe I pose a threat to anyone. My height is my height, and I can't do anything about that.

There is another episode I would like to share with you about this topic. I once attended a dinner party at a co-worker's house many years ago. As I was walking into the house, I noticed an African American man was staring at me. He introduced himself and offered me to sit down. (At the time, I did not know he was the hostess' husband until much later). We both sat and started to chat a bit. In the middle of our conservation, he made an interesting statement and an unorthodox analogy: He stated, "When you see a gorilla walking into a room, you don't expect him to sit down and carry on an intelligent conservation." At the time, I did not realize he was talking about me. When I have shared this encounter with friends, they felt it was an odd way to pay someone a compliment. I guess I was too naïve to realize this man's analogy was a "compliment." Obviously, his analogy went over my head. What's my point? My point is that all people make perceptions. Regardless they are accurate or far-fetched, people will make judgments and perceptions about each other, which I believe is unfortunate and prosperous!

Do you recall me stating that there are numerous social diseases we have in America? Perceptions fall in this category, too. People make and form perceptions all the time. Unfortunately, this is not good, because perceptions are not necessarily valid, and they can be negative and offensive. Some perceptions have been established centuries and continue to exist in our society. I believe in order to dispel perceptions of African Americans, our society needs to change its way of thinking about African Americans. When people put themselves in other people's shoes, they tend to look at things differently. No one wants to be treated unfairly and/or badly. No one wants to be discriminated against. No one wants to live in fear. No one wants to be followed in stores or by the police while driving, because of his or her skin color or ethnicity. No one wants to be discriminated against because of the color of his or her skin. I believe if non-African Americans did not think like this, there is a great possibility of minimizing perceptions and *racism* in America. Just so I am clear, I am not suggesting and claiming this will stop people from making perceptions or being racist. However, this is a good start to have Americans to develop a different mindset of African Americans.

Why Do Americans Hate Americans?

CHAPTER 17

African American Mothers Raise Their Daughters and Spoil Their Sons

Years ago, I read an article in a magazine about how African American mothers reared their daughters and spoiled their sons. The article intrigued me, because I had never heard this before, and I didn't realize that African American mothers were rearing their children this way. In my family, it was just the opposite. My mother pretty much trained me to clean the house, wash dishes, sweep and mop the floors, scrub the walls, wash clothes and iron them. In addition, she would send me on errands to pay bills downtown Chicago. We had a Sunbeam iron that would occasionally stop working. My mom would send me to the West Side of Chicago to the Sunbeam factory to have the iron fixed. Just so you know, I was in the fourth grade making these trips by myself, as well as traveling from the South Side of Chicago via public transportation. My younger sister and brother had it made. They were not relied on that much to do house chores or errands. Even though my brother is just a year younger than I am and my sister is three years younger, my mother did not depend on them that much. Since I was the oldest of the three, a lot of responsibility was commissioned to me. I was also responsible for the safety and well-being of my two siblings, when my parents were not at home.

When I became an adolescent, I started to notice that my male friends were not doing house chores that I was doing since I was 8 years old. This made me a bit sour and resentful. I confronted them about this, and they just laughed at me. I could not understand why their mothers did not have them do more house chores.

Getting back to the article I read, it pointed out some interesting things about how the African American mothers were rearing their daughters and sons differently. For example, the article reported that these mothers trained their daughters how to balance a checkbook, cook and clean house, handle money and take care of themselves. In contrast, the boys were not trained how to balance a checkbook, cook and clean house, handle money and take care of themselves. Instead, their mothers were doing practically everything for them. I can attest to this, because many of my male friends had mothers who took care of them as opposed to rearing them like their sisters. I know some people believe that girls and boys are different. Therefore, they should be reared differently. I disagree. Yes, there are differences between girls and boys regarding physical characteristics and physiology, but everyone needs to know how to take care of herself and himself when she or he becomes an adult. Period. I do not believe it is in the best interests of boys not knowing about <u>personal responsibility</u> and learning life skills.

It is unfortunate that a significant number of African American boys, if not the majority, as well as African American girls, are reared without fathers in their households. However, this does not preclude African American boys from receiving proper training, helping them to become responsible individuals with character. According to the research I have reviewed and studied, the majority of African American juveniles are from families without their biological fathers. Moreover, many of these juveniles do not know or never met their <u>biological</u> fathers. This is the same case with African American men who are in jail or prison.

Racism has been implicated in African American men's lives in reference to them being unable and/or incapable of assuming their paternal responsibility. I have heard many African American men blaming "the system" for their predicament. What these men are saying is that it is not their fault not being able to take care of their children and personal responsibilities. Perhaps there may be some validity to this, but I am not too sure if it is that "black and white" or if there is a cause and effect phenomenon involved. I really cannot elaborate much on this, because I do not know African American men who have been victimized by "the system." The African American fathers I know take care of business, including caring for their children and families.

I would be remiss if I did not mention African American fathers who fathered children. These fathers should be held responsible for their paternal obligations, too. Just because you can father a child does not mean you are a responsible father. (There is a difference between being a father and being a responsible father). It is inexcusable for African American fathers not to financially support their children and being involved in their lives in a healthy way.

Fathers are extremely important in their children's lives. Research studies show that children whose fathers are actively and responsibly in their lives tend to do well in school, are less likely to get in trouble with the law, and are likely to have healthy relationships. Unfortunately, this is not the case for a significant number of African Americans children. I completed my dissertation on bonding between African American youths and their fathers. Without saying, African American youths need their father in their lives. African American mothers can only do so much, and they definitely cannot be male role models for their children, especially for their sons!

Since becoming an adult, I have always long to seek my father's advice regarding *racism* and being an African American man. There were numerous times I desperately needed my father's advice, but he was never available. This created a void in my life. As a result of this, my experience with *racism* and striving to become a man was based on trials and errors. Unfortunately, I had made some regrettable mistakes, which have caused me a tremendous amount of despair and anguish. Even today, I am still paying for these mistakes I made in my life. Of course, I cannot blame anyone for the choices I made in my life. Nevertheless, I strongly believe if my father were present in my life when I was a teenager, my life would have been drastically different now!

Why Do Americans Hate Americans?

Reflection

_____

_____

_____

_____

_____

_____

_____

_____

_____

_____

_____

_____

_____

_____

_____

CHAPTER 18

A Man's Conscience is His Worst Enemy

I believe a man's conscience is his worst enemy, and the same could be said for a woman's, too. Hence, I guess I could say that <u>our</u> conscience is our worst enemy. I was having this conversation with my mother years ago. She believes that some people do not have a conscience. I disagreed. I believe everyone has a conscience and that people, in general, are aware of and know the difference between right from wrong. My mother was making references to her personal life experiences and living during the *Jim Crow era*. During this time, she and her family and relatives experienced *racism*, hatred, *discrimination* and evil. I was coming from an academic and spiritual perspective. I don't believe there is a right or wrong view of this topic. However, I would like to expand on the matter.

When I was in graduate school, I studied the id, ego and superego (conscience). According to Sigmund Freud, the id, ego and superego consist of the structure of our personality as human beings. Freud postulates that there is a constant battle among the three tenets. I am not going to spend a lot time on psychoanalysis. I just wanted to provide a platform.

Of course, my mother knows what she is talking about, because she lived through some horrendous times; times that I cannot fathom that ever existed in the human race, especially in the United States of America where all citizens are supposed to be freed and treated equally and fairly. According to my mother, *racism* was rampant during her life in Alabama. Blacks were not allowed to share the same public facilities such as water fountains and restrooms with whites. Blacks were not allowed to eat at the counters in restaurants; the counters were reserved for "whites only." Some restaurants and hotels prohibited blacks from entering their front doors; they were only allowed to enter hotels and certain restaurants through the back door. (This included professional African American athletes, singers, movie stars). Even though blacks and whites paid the same bus fare, blacks were required to sit in the back of the bus. In some cases, blacks were required to give up their seats, if the white-only section was filled. Blacks were also required to sit in the balcony of white theaters and white churches. Blacks were not allowed to visit or live in certain neighborhoods, where all whites lived. Blacks were not allowed to have certain jobs. School integration was illegal.

Some people believe things have changed. I am not too sure about this, when we still have *racism, discrimination* and *bigotry* in America. Some people believe that African Americans do not have the same issues that their ancestors endured. To some extent, this might be *partially* true. As I mentioned earlier in this book, we have the *hate crime law* which did not exist during my mother's time. I suspect that some people want to believe that blacks today are better off than their ancestors. Of course, there are no public lynchings, as they were often the norm decades ago. In fact, they were popular, to the point that some white families brought their children to watch with picnic baskets. Cross burnings are still a reality in America; racial profiling happens every day in America; and corporations, businesses and employers are sued often because of *institutional* and *systemic racism* and *discrimination*.

I believe some people refuse to make themselves aware of *racism* in America. Some people know that *racism* exists in America, but they do not want to acknowledge the right and wrong (conscience) issues related to *racism* in our country. Perhaps this is where my mother's statement about some people do not have a conscience is valid. In contrast, I believe our conscience cannot be ignored or denied. Before an individual tries to destroy his or her own conscience, he or she might just annihilate himself or herself. This shows the power of our conscience.

Spiritually, our conscience reminds us what is right and wrong, but it is about choices we make in life. Everyone has the volition to exert his or her free will to make choices. However, there are always consequences and repercussions for our actions. For example, a racist person may not believe he or she is wrong in hurting and killing African Americans, but a racist must live with his or her conscience or *guilty conscience*. Perhaps racist people might go to their graves with their taunting conscience, knowing that they have hurt, and in some cases, killed blacks because of their race. Moreover, racist groups such as the KKK read the same Bible some African American Christians read, yet there is so much evil and hatred displayed by the KKK and racist groups toward African Americans. In fact, KKK members claimed they have killed in the name of God, but it is not the same god who is about love, peace, kindness, forgiveness and justice for all. Amazing! This is why I believe a person's conscience is his or her worst enemy.

Why Do Americans Hate Americans?

CHAPTER 19

Police Officers vs. African American Men: As it Relates to Racism

To serve and protect and do no harm is the oath doctors, attorneys, educators, ministers, health professors, public officials and police officers have taken when they were sworn into office. This oath is supreme and paramount. Americans have entrusted the public officials and civil servants with their lives and trust. When the aforementioned oath has been violated by trusting professionals, it causes distrust and disbelief, delivering a devastating blow to one's psychic, soul and spirit. There is nothing more demoralizing and hurtful to see than white male police officers beating and killing black men whom they are supposed to serve and protect. In America, it has become common to see videos and news coverages showing white male police officers choking, kicking, pinning down, and beating black men to their death. What is so fascinating is that the media, which continue ignite and fuel *racism*, often, show these occurrences. Sometimes there are protests, which create more violence and hatred. It seems there is no end to these public "*lynchings*." I use this word, because I see no difference between what I have seen the KKK members have done to black men with a rope and what white male police officers have done with their sticks and guns to black men.

Please understand I am not saying that all white male police officers are guilty of these heinous crimes; just the ones who have been video-recorded, or shown on news, choking, kicking, clubbing and killing black men.

A few days ago, I was watching CNN journalists Don Lemon and Chris Cuomo discussing an incident in Minneapolis, Minnesota, involving a white male police officer pinning down a black man with his knee. The black man eventfully died. As I was watching the coverage, Don Lemon, who is an African American man, was expressing his personal dislike about the incident to his colleague, Chris Cuomo, who is an Italian American. It was obvious that this dialogue was not staged. Don Lemon was quite upset and extremely outspoken about *racism* in America, and Chris Cuomo was listening respectfully and intensively. This is my very first time watching a news coverage about a white male police officer killing a black man that was not was staged or rehearsed. I could not believe how blunt Don Lemon was with Chris Cuomo. This was live news coverage. We need more news coverage like this, exposing police brutality and *racism* in America. Fascinating!

I believe when the media are transparent about *racism* in America, this will enable Americans to start having dialogues and conversations about this social disease in our country. As I stated previously, whites and blacks are not discussing *racism* collectively, collaboratively and civilly.

There are too many laws, legislation and policies that do not have any bite. I do not believe there will ever be sufficient, effective laws, legislation and policies that will have an impact on *racism* in America. <u>Americans need to solve this social issue themselves</u>!

Racism is a societal problem; and it is a maladaptive behavior problem. Our society needs to help educate and train police officers how to diffuse *racism* in America. One of the main problems we have with *racism* is perception. (Remember I mentioned earlier that perception is based on prejudice, prejudging without the facts). One of the common denominators I often see in cases like the one that occurred in Minneapolis, Minnesota is the stature of the African American male. Usually, African American men who are tall and big are perceived to be intimidating. I am tall, but not big, yet I am told that my height is intimidating to some people. Sometimes just the presence of African American men make people uneasy, cringe and scared. Chicago has a city ordinance prohibiting groups of people from gathering on street corners. Mainly, young African American men are seen gathering on street corners in Chicago. This makes some people uncomfortable and intimidated.

People are wondering why there is protesting, looting and riots are occurring in our country now. As I stated earlier, unsolved issues from the past affect the future and present. George Floyd's death and other deaths of African Americans are not the only cause of people protesting in the streets in America. Chronic *systemic racism* is the cause, as well as *institutional and structural racism*, injustice, unfairness, and inequity. (Just for the record, I do not, do not condone violence, killing, looting or stealing, but I do condemn *racism* and hatred). I do understand some of the reasons why Americans are protesting, but I do not agree with some of the activities I have observed on TV.

Americans must realize that *racism* just doesn't affect African Americans. It affects all Americans! Period. Of course, we know that *racism* has an adverse effect on African Americans' lives, but it also has an effect on our entire country. When people become fed up, broken and feeling hopeless and helpless, they are likely to give up on hope and become disruptive and suicidal. The underlying issues of suicide is hopelessness and helplessness. These are the feelings of <u>some</u> Americans.

During the 1968 riots, I was 13 years old, and in the eighth grade. It was an extraordinarily violent time. People were looting, rioting and dying. We had curfews in Chicago. I saw military tanks riding down the streets in my neighborhood, causing a state of unrest. Everything was in a turmoil. Richard J. Daley issued the order to "shoot to kill" any looters. Suddenly, the looting came to a complete halt. President Donald Trump has made comments in the same context. When Richard J. Daley gave the order to shoot to kill looters, I do not recall anyone calling him a racist. Interesting!

As I am writing this book, America is in an uproar due to the police killing of George Floyd and racial injustice. Right now, there seems to be no relief in sight. People are still protesting, and some people are still looting and dying. Just last week 22 people were killed in Chicago over the weekend. Chicago has never had so many people killed on a weekend.

I am receiving calls from friends who are completely scared and depressed, because of the protests in their neighborhoods and the constant siren noises. They have not seen so much destruction and property damage in their lives. For some of them, this is their very first time witnessing the despair in their communities and throughout the United States of America.

In Buffalo, New York 57 police officers resigned from the riot unit in a show of support for two colleagues who were suspended after they were filmed shoving an elderly man to the ground during looting and violence. I can only imagine police officers are dealing with a situation for which they are not prepared. As I stated previously, all police officers are not the same. There are some good ones, and there are some bad ones. I have relatives and friends who are police officers, and I have the utmost respect and admiration for them. I love them all!

With all what is going on in America, I do not see how much longer police officers and the American people will be able to continue to endure and sustain. Human beings can endure, only so much. Our economy is still struggling; the unemployment rate is still high; many businesses are still closed and/or partially opened; and a significant number of people are without resources. Moreover, at the current time of writing this book, there are over 30 million Americans who are unemployed, and a significant number of them are not receiving unemployment. Although president Trump asked that landlords and creditors to be lenient and understanding, but some people have been evicted from their apartments and homes. Understandably, landlords and creditors have bills, too, and financial obligations to meet. However, no one seems to be showing any sympathy or compassion during these challenging times. Unfortunately, there is some exploitation and price gouging, during this pandemic and unrest in America. I have noticed some business owners and merchants have doubled up on their prices for their goods and services and merchandise. For instance, prior to the pandemic, some barbers were charging $15 for a basic haircut. Now some of them are charging $25 for the same haircut. No one is giving anyone a break on anything during these tough times.

With the combination of COVID-19 and the protests, African Americans will be pressured more to find ways to survive. Like everyone else, African Americans want to survive and live fulfilling lives. Unfortunately, this will be difficult for many of them due to fear and distrust many of them have toward police officers. Lately, various TV shows have interviewed African American fathers regarding the safety of their children's lives, especially their sons'. African American fathers are painfully concerned, because they know that they and their sons are endangered species.

Years ago, I had a discussion with several of my African American male friends who have sons. I asked these fathers how they are preparing their sons, when they have contact with police officers. In response, the majority of them said that they have trained their sons to be respectful, polite and courteous toward police officers, because they did not want their sons dead. I believe this is the mindset for many, if not the majority, of African Americans fathers with sons. No one wants his or her children to die at the hands of a police officer. When will this all end?

Why Do Americans Hate Americans?

<u>Reflection</u>

_____

_____

_____

_____

_____

_____

_____

_____

_____

_____

_____

_____

_____

CHAPTER 20

In God We Trust

America was built on the foundation of God. "In God We Trust" is on American currencies; this religious phrase used to be posted and seen in courtrooms, municipalities and government buildings for years. We used to use the word God in the Pledge to Allegiance to the American flag. But now anything that mentions or written using the word God is prohibited, especially in public and government facilities. God has been removed from our public schools, social gatherings and meetings. People want to separate church and state. As a result, there has been chaos and confusion in every aspect of America.

Interestingly, when 9/11 happened, churches, synagogues and mosques were filled, and Americans were calling on God for intervention and redemption. This only lasted a few months, and people went back to "business as usual."

In 2020, America was afflicted by COVID-19, but this time people cannot go to the churches, synagogues or mosque to worship, due to the lockdown across the United States of America. In addition, we also have the protests, looting and riots. America is on fire, but fire purifies and brings a newness to life. It is just a matter of time. However, Americans cannot expect things will be like they used to be prior to the pandemic and protests. America needs a new spirit. America needs a new attitude. America will need a new people of races.

When catastrophes strike, Americans call out to God. People want to blame God for all the wrongs they have caused. God does not cause catastrophes; God does not cause evil; God does not cause greed or fear; God does not cause hatred; and God is not the cause for *racism* in America. We serve a loving God who is merciful and caring. America has been pulling away from God for years. God never left America; America left God!

Personally, I do not see a way out of this darkness without the help of God. God is the Way, the Truth and the Life. He is the only One who can get America out of this darkness. If America really wants to find its way out of this mess, Americans need to repent and ask God for forgiveness and mercy. There is so much evil in the world, especially in the United States of America. Evil has no power over God. God is the only One who has control over the entire world and evil. America, we need to call on God and stay faithful and loyal to Him. We cannot expect Him to be a magic wand every time we are in a bind. Americans need to trust God, in the same way we trust Him with our money: *"In God We Trust."*

America has a choice to trust God. America has a choice to call on God for help. America has a choice to submit to the will of God. What America is seeing and experiencing is not the will of God. The unrest and COVID-19 are caused by man, not by God. God has given man the free will to make choices. With those choices, there are consequences. No action comes without a reaction.

Why Do Americans Hate Americans?

CHAPTER 21

What Does Love Got to Do with Racism?

What does love got to do with *racism*? Well, it has a lot to do with it! Love is the greatest gift of all. Without love, there is no peace. Without love, there is no harmony among the American people. Without love, there cannot be any progress. Without love, *racism* will continue to be a wedge between blacks and whites. Love is the only antidote that will fix America's racial and people problems.

The word love is a verb; a verb is an action word. Love is about action. If you really love someone, you put your love into action. For example, when a spouse loves his or her spouse, he or she will show it by his or her action.

It is OK to tell someone you love her or him, but it is more impacting to put your words into action. A nice gift, a gentle touch, a compliment, or service are ways to express your love toward your loved one. Likewise, black people need to feel that they are loved by white people and vice versa.

In order to eradicate *racism* in America, Americans need to love each other. Of course, it is easier said than done. This is what makes it intriguing and challenging.

Love is patience and kindness. Love is caring, empathy, sympathy, compassion, and giving. In order to receive love, you much give it first. Love is not earned like many people believe. Love is a gift from God; God is love.

When you love someone, you are committed, meaning you will do anything and everything for that person. Blacks have learned how to love America, but America has not learned how to love blacks. Many blacks have lost their lives building this country. Many blacks have given their sweat and tears for the sake of this country. Now is the time for America to give back to blacks, starting with love!

I have an acronym for L.O.V.E.:

L= Life

O= Omniscient, Omnipotent, Omnipresent

V= Victory

E= Everyone

Everyone wants to be loved and receive love. I strongly believe that the protests will come to a complete halt, when love is permeated throughout America. Americans are dying to be loved. Love conquers all!

Why Do Americans Hate Americans?

<u>Reflection</u>

_____

_____

_____

_____

_____

_____

_____

_____

_____

_____

_____

_____

_____

_____

CHAPTER 22

Redefining America: As it Relates to Racism

America is in turmoil right now. There is so much confusion and uncertainty about its future and the American people. Not only is America dealing with the COVID-19 pandemic, it is also dealing with the riots, demonstrations, protests, looting and killings of African American men. Initially, when I first started writing this book, I had no idea I would be writing about a pandemic and racial upheaval in America. Every day I am learning something new from the media related to *racism* in America. Now there have been numerous discussions about changing laws and policies and implementing new laws and policies related to *racism* in America. I am not sure if people are genuinely listening, or they are just going through the motions.

Personally, I do not believe it is realistic to expect drastic changes to occur overnight. There is a lot of history, or should I say, a lot of *dead* history involved. To expect American history to be rewritten and changed overnight is not realistic!

Redefining America is more than a notion. There are talks and discussions about changing and removing virtually everything, including Confederate statues, Confederate monuments, slave owners' legacies, portraits and symbols that represented *racism* and slavery in the American history. Oh boy, this is something to see, if it comes to past.

Blacks want changes now! Changes that would redefine and transform America and give Americans a new identity to the world, as this probably would be expected. Though, this new identity probably would not be recognizable to the world. This new identity probably will change the road map to a different destiny for America and its people. This new identity will redefine the term *democracy*. *Democracy* will mean the same for all Americans, both in theory and practice. Right now *democracy* means different things for different people. We only live in a democratic society in theory, but not in practicality. Our democratic society does not recognize or treat all Americans equally, fairly, equitably, civilly or respectfully, especially black Americans. We live in a *democracy* in name only.

Historically, Americans wanted to be independent from the federal government. When the government regulates and controls everything, it is extraordinarily costly and everything is centralized, meaning that our federal government makes decisions independently and regulates the people. Now, Americans want the federal government to provide structure, guidance, direction and leadership, making it more decentralized and bureaucratic. Currently, I see the federal government and local governments are reluctant to embrace the latter. We see this with our current president, during the pandemic crisis. He is suggesting that the local governors provide the structure, guidance, direction and leadership to their respective states. Interestingly, the governors do not seem to be willing to do this, without financial support from the White House.

I have been listening to many talk shows and watching news coverage about both the COVID-19 pandemic and *racism*. There seems to be immense focus on changes, reforming policing and changing policies and laws so that "Black Lives Matter" becomes a reality. College professors, ministers, authors, public officials and consultants have been discussing methods and ways to implement changes. However, nothing seems to be put in action at this time. One of the positive things about all of this is that people are talking about changes. People are talking about changing America, and people are talking about changing themselves.

I agree with what I have heard from college professors, ministers and some public officials. They suggest that it is going to take a multicultural of people to bring about changes in America. Every ethnic group, Women's groups, and the LGBTQ community need to be <u>actively</u> involved in this *evolution* taking place in America. We do not need more policies and laws; we need action! Things need to be in place so that America can change. Otherwise, all the protests and demonstrations would be in vain.

I was on the phone with my former college buddy who lives in Japan. He and I were on Skype approximately 4 hours, discussing the unrest in America and COVID-

19. By the way, he is white. I would like to share some things we talked about regarding *racism*. I must admit this was the very first time we had a transparent, stimulating and heartfelt discussion about racial issues and *racism* in America. Previously, *racism* was a topic that we would not discuss for various reasons. Today was a different story. Prior to the call, I was wondering if any of my white friends would call me, to discuss *racism*, especially given the circumstances facing black men in America. After all I am an African American man. Thus far, my friend from Japan is the only one who has called me. He had so much to share with me about his "racist friends," and I had a lot to share with him about my victimization of *racism*, including being profiled on numerous occasions. There was no blaming involved. As I wrote previously, white people do not like being blamed for what their ancestors have done to African Americans. They will

shut down and become defensive, if you blame them for the chronic and historical *racism* that existed in America for centuries. Apparently, my friend felt compelled to call me about what he had been watching on TV about white police officers killing black men and his conversations with his "racist friends." I must admit that our four-hour conversation was quite intense and excitable, but with respect and without malice.

To my surprise, I learned that my buddy has been trying to educate his "racist friends" about African Americans, particularly African American men. Many of his "racist friends" despise African Americans and think very poorly of us. In spite of my buddy's rebuttal, his "racist friends" are adamant that African Americans are pretty much the way we are portrayed by the media and by the negative images seen in movies and ads. This is so unfortunate. Even when <u>some</u> white people are given *accurate* information about African Americans, they still insist on believing the stereotypes, misconceptions and preconceived notions about us. This makes me wonder if <u>some</u> white people will ever be able to change their ways of thinking about African Americans. If this is the case, it is going to be extremely difficult to make strides during these momentous times. I believe we need more than the majority of American people to inspire changes.

This is my second time witnessing an unrest in America, particularly in Chicago. During the 1960s, when Dr. Martin King was assassinated, America was in upheaval with riots, lootings and killings. I witnessed military tanks driving through my neighborhood and National guards posted outside of stores and businesses. We also had a curfew. After the late Chicago mayor Richard J. Daley gave the orders to shot to kill looters, the looting came to a complete halt. Once the smoke cleared, the West Side of Chicago was destroyed. There were ruins, debris and remnants from the lootings and fires. As of today, the West Side of Chicago has not been completely rebuilt. There are some pockets where you can see some rebuilding done, but there is still a lot of rebuilding needs to be done on the West Side of Chicago.

This unrest is a bit different, but similar in some ways. For instance, the life of a black man was taken by a white police officer, sparking protests, looting and more killings of African Americans. Not only did a black man lose his life, there were other African Americans whose lives were lost in the midst of this unrest and prior to the unrest.

Black baby boomers may have a different perspective of the situation compared to black millennials and black Generation X individuals. Black baby boomers experienced a lot more than black millennials and black Generation X people, during the riots in 1964. Things were much worst during the Civil Rights Movement and prior to the Civil Rights Movement for blacks. Not only there were killings, but there also were numerous lynchings across the nation. The infamous Emmett Till murder was horrendous and the epitome of evil and hatred toward black boys and black men. The child was beaten to a pulp and lynched; he was only 14 years old and a native of Chicago. Interestingly, blacks did not take to the streets, as they have today. I can only speculate that the Emmett Till's murder and the assassinations of Dr. King and Malcolm X ignited the 1964 riots in America. Blacks were saying enough is enough! Sadly, not much came from the riots. There were only changes on papers, but white people's behavior did not change. America continues to have racial issues between blacks and whites.

America has a short memory or living in denial of all the young black lives have been lost at the hands of white people, especially white police officers killing black boys and black men. George Floyd is not the only reason blacks have taken to the streets, protesting and demanding for changes. Blacks who have lost their lives prior to the killing of George Floyd and during the unrest is the reason blacks have turned to the streets. The world is watching America, to see whether it does the right thing; and that is to change the way it has been treating blacks.

Not only do blacks want to see changes, but the world wants to see changes, too. It is no secret how white people have been mistreating blacks in America.

In order to redefine America, *black-on-black crime* needs to be addressed and resolved, too. As I have stated previously, *black-on-black crime* is just as serious as *racism* in America. Both are considered to be social diseases. Hence, there is no cure, but they can be treated, provided that <u>all</u> Americans are invested and committed to finding antidotes for these two diseases. I do not believe *racism* will be impacted until some black people value life and themselves. When white Americans see that black people value themselves and life, this will definitely have an impact on how white America perceives and treats black America. This is not a black problem, but an American problem. We all are in this together as a race, the human race. Period.

Why Do Americans Hate Americans?

CHAPTER 23

Diversity vs. Multiculturism: As it Relates to Racism

The United States of America is a diverse country. As I mentioned previously, all walks of lives and ethnic races are represented in America. *Diversity* has been the focus for America for the past few decades. Some people believe *diversity* is the way to go. Even the American government encourages businesses, organizations, corporations, colleges and universities to be diverse in their hiring, as well as among their employees and staff members. Although *diversity* sounds great, I believe it causes more division than unity and solitary. I have seen *diversity* in my own workplace for approximately 10 years, yet employees were divided and antisocial. Based on my observation, the African Americans preferred to socialize with African Americans; the Mexican Americans preferred to socialize with Mexican Americans; the non-African Americans preferred to socialize with non-African Americans; and the Asian Americans preferred to socialize with Asian Americans. It seems that people prefer to socialize with people who are like them, with similar backgrounds, languages, cultures, music, food, traditions, etc. I did not see that much socializing among this diverse group on my job. Instead, I saw Americans socializing with their "own kind." *Diversity* is not necessarily a bad or good thing; it is just a *principle* that the American government has encouraged and supported. I am not sure how this concept came about, but it does not have that much substance or true meaning. This is my opinion, based on my professional experiences working with people.

In contrast, *multiculturalism* has been part of the American culture for quite some time. In fact, when I was attending graduate school to become a therapist, it was required that I take multicultural courses with the goal of learning about other ethnic groups and races differ from minds.

The multicultural approach seems to have more meaning and significance. There are books written about *multiculturalism*. In its infancy, very little was known about *multiculturalism*. Now, there is plethora of literature and information about it. This is the not case with *diversity*. What is my point? My point is that I believe there should be more focus and emphasis on *multiculturalism* than *diversity*.

Multiculturalism is related to all aspects of races, ethnic groups and nationalities. For instance, people's ethnicities, customs, traditions, etc. should be acknowledged and used in their relationships with each other. This can have an impact on *racism* in America. If Americans place themselves in other people's shoes, they will have a better understanding of these individuals' trials, tribulations, and plight. For example, if white people allowed themselves to assume the role of blacks, they will learn more about what is it like being black living in America. A person cannot have an appreciation of another person's life, unless he or she is walking in that person's shoes. Of course, I am not suggesting that white people should pretend to be black or vice versa. However, altruism, sensitivity, empathy, sympathy, compassion, caring and love can make a difference in human behavior. These are all attributes innately in our DNA. It is just a matter of allowing them to broaden our consciousness and awareness. This is the time America needs to utilize the multicultural approach in all facets of our country.

In order for America to emerge from this darkness, it needs to embrace the multicultural approach, meaning that people need to begin to think about others' predicament and situation as if it were their own. For example, when black people suffer, the entire country suffers. This is not about a black and white issue; it is all about the American people --- supporting, caring, loving and respecting each other regardless. Period. America has the resources; America has the manpower; America has the ability; and America has the people. This is what *multiculturalism* is all about!

It has been my experience that multicultural approach has a positive effect on human behavior. People tend to behave and think differently, when all races, creeds, colors, nationalities are involved in social issues affecting people in general. The "Black Lives Matter" movement can benefit from the multicultural approach. A multicultural of people has the power, influence, and resources that are not necessarily evident with one particular race or ethnic group. By having a multicultural of people involved, the group tends to be more involved, invested and efficacious!

Why Do Americans Hate Americans?

CHAPTER 24

Black America vs. White America

As an African American living in America, oftentimes it feels and seems like I am living in two separate countries simultaneously. The laws are different for African Americans, even though they are written for all Americans. For example, the federal laws for illegal drugs in black neighborhoods are enforced and interpreted differently compared to the white suburbs. African Americans are prosecuted more harshly than non-African Americans. The impact of COVID-19 is significantly different for African Americans due to the lack of resources and support in the black communities, as evidenced by the unrest and economic depression and rampant crime. African

Americans are two times more likely to be profiled than non-African Americans. The due process is often ignored for African Americans than whites. One of the reasons for this is that 80% to 90% blacks do not know the components of the due process: 1.). The right to cross-examine your accuser(s). 2.). The right to legal representation. If you cannot afford an attorney, the court will appoint one. 3.). The right to remain silent. 4.). The right to a speedy trial. 5.). The right to be notified of charges. It is my belief that police officers know that the average African American does not know his or her rights, particularly the due process. Therefore, the probability of African Americans being *railroaded* in the court of law is very high. In contrast, the average white person is unlikely to be railroaded, because he or she can afford an attorney, and some police officers tend to treat whites differently from African Americans in reference to the law and criminal activities. This is based on my professional and personal experience working with the public.

During the unrest, I have noticed that things have not changed that much for African Americans, especially for African American males. Being an African American male, I sense some resentment from some whites when I am in the public shopping or dining at restaurants. It is the same feelings I experienced prior to the unrest. Some whites give off negative vibes or stares, making you feel unwelcomed or despised. I know the media have been advocating unity and solidarity, but I do not feel this when I am in the presence of some whites. I would like to share a story with you. There is a restaurant I used to dine at in Elmhurst, Illinois. It was a Greek restaurant. One day as I was paying for my meal, the owner said to me: "Be a good boy. Be a good boy." I was totally surprised and appalled by his statement and did not know what he meant by it. I really wanted to question him. Instead, I decided to pay for my meal and leave. I did not know the owner other than coming into his restaurant to eat. We never talked about politics or the unrest in America. He was always friendly and courteous. After this incident, there was another time I went to this restaurant to eat. I wanted to question the owner about his previous statement, but again I did not. My spirit would not allow me to approach him. This was the last time I ate at the restaurant. Sometimes it is best to leave things alone and let the Holy Spirit fight your battles. This was one of those cases I listened to the Holy Spirit. The sad part about this is that I really enjoyed the food and service there. As we know, everything happens for a reason(s).

Not everything is black and white as some people want to believe. As I mentioned previously, America is a diverse country. However, everyone is not treated the same regarding fairness, justice, equitability and equity. Unfortunately, race has a tremendous effect on how people are serviced in restaurants and hotels, treated by police officers and business people and the public. In general, people are judged by their appearance, attire, and skin color. Before a person says a word, he or she is judged on his or her appearance. Now, if the person is non-African American, waiting to be serviced in a store or restaurant, it is likely that he or she will be given the utmost respect and services, whereas an African American would not have the same experience. Even though both have similar socioeconomic status (SES) and education, but different skin color, there will be a difference in how both are treated and addressed by store clerks, restaurant servers, agents, customer service, etc. There have been countless occasions where I was waiting first in line to be served by a white clerk and the clerk would completely bypass me to serve a white customer. Of course, I would let the white clerk know that I was first in line to be served. Now, what is so interesting about these occasions is that I have never experienced where the white customer would speak up, letting the white clerk know that he or she was in error. In fact, some white customers have attempted to be served before me until I interrupt. Incidents like these cause and/or precipitate chaos and confusion in America, as well as a division and polarization between whites and blacks.

I do not believe White America perceives Black America as an asset to the American economy. It is my belief that some white Americans believe that the majority of African Americans are on public aid, receiving government assistance for food, shelter and medical care. This is further from the truth. The majority of public aid recipients are white people. In fact, based on the research I have reviewed, approximately 66% of African Americans are middle-class. Another fact is that African Americans are major consumers. We spend billions of dollars on goods and services, including but not limited to, purchases of homes, automobiles, real estate property, college tuition, etc. Now what is unfortunate is that some African Americans do not invest or spend their money wisely, giving the impression that we are a financial burden to the White America. I must admit I do not know the magnitude of this issue, but I do know many African Americans are doing well, financially, in America.

I have a story to share with you. When I first attained my doctorate, I was having a conversation with a restaurant owner who was Greek. During our conversation, he made an interesting statement to me. He stated, "Now you can help your own people." In response, I told him that I took an oath to serve and protect and do no harm, meaning that I am commissioned to help all Americans regardless of their creed, nationality, ethnicity, religion, customs, SES, etc. In response, he stated, "Yeah, but you still need to help your people." I do not believe there was any malice behind his statements. In fact, his sister and my niece were best of friends, while they were in grade school and high school. Also, I knew their parents, so this person was a decent human being, as well as his family. Nevertheless, I am always reflecting on our conversation and the context of it. The more I think about the conversation, I can better understand his thinking. I believe this may be typical thinking of majority of whites in America, meaning whites help their people and blacks should help their people. This seems a bit paradoxical, since we are all Americans and live in America. Hence, Americans should help each other regardless. Period. Perhaps I am being naïve, but I strongly believe Americans should look at each other as one race, under God, indivisible, with liberty and justice for all! At least these words are part of the American Pledge to Allegiance.

In reality, each ethnic group primarily helps its own people, with the exception of African Americans. Sadly, but this is a fact. There is so much dissension and division among African Americans. I am quite sure blacks will not like reading this, but it is a fact. I have often heard other African Americans using the analogy: "We are like a barrel of crabs; no one gets to the top, because we are so busy pulling each other down." It is extraordinarily painful for me to admit this, but I have witnessed this, and I have been victimized by this. Blacks can be their own worst enemy!

White America is aware of the internal problems Black America is encountering, especially black-on-black crime. I strongly believe if Black America were able to overcome this challenge, the majority of our issues will be resolved. However, White America's help is badly needed, in order to eradicate this chronic social disease. As I mentioned earlier, Black America does not have the resources, support or tools to resolve this issue, independently. I know some blacks would disagree, and I welcome any argument on this issue!

For the past several decades, the demographics of America has changed. For instance, the *baby boomers* (babies born between 1946 and 1964) were the fastest and largest segment of the American population. During the *baby boomer* era, approximately 76 million babies were born in the United States of America. The *baby boomers* recreated the American economy and lifestyle. Prior to World War II, our society was industrialized, and the majority of Americans lived on farms and did agricultural work and hard labor. After World War II, America became an information and service society, making this era prosperous and solvent. Even now, *baby boomers* are believed to be much more prosperous than their predecessors or previous generations.

African American *baby boomers* are quite different from their predecessors such as African American *Generation X* individuals and African American *millennials* in reference to consumerism, consumption of goods and services, spirituality, social issues, family values and work ethic. Obviously, *baby boomers* are older than *Generation X* cohorts and *millennials*. By living longer and experiencing an array of social issues and *racism* in one's lifespan, African American *baby boomers* are likely to have gained more wisdom, knowledge and insight about *racism*. Specifically, during the riots in 1964, African American *baby boomers* may have endured a lot more of anguish and agony than their predecessors. For instance, there were more reports of lynching, killings of African Americans, especially African Americans men. The rioting and looting were more intense and devastating in 1964 compared to the looting and rioting now. The *Black Panthers* were actively involved in the Civil Rights moments. Now there are no reports of *Black Panthers*. My reason for mentioning the _Black Panthers_ is that the American government considered them as "communists," as well as the late Dr. Martin Luther King, Jr. However, what separated the Black Panthers from other civil rights leaders and activists was that the *Panthers* were armed and dangerous. They did not take any mess!

From 1965 to 1980, the *Generation X* was born. During this time, approximately 65 million babies were born. This generation is not as prosperous as the *baby boomer* generation. Hence, a significant number of African American *Generation* X people and African

American *millennials* depend on their parents for financial support. In fact, many African American *Generation X* individuals and African American *millennials* still live with their parents, as well as these individuals' children who are the grandchildren of African American *baby boomers*. Economically, it is extremely difficult for African Americans to make a living in America without the help from others. I believe there are two reasons for this. Of course, *racism* has a lot to do with it, as well as the work ethic. Regarding the latter, I do not believe African Americans of the *Generation X* and *millennial* eras are willing to endure the type of treatment and injustice African American *baby boomers* endured for so many decades. I don't believe African Americans of the *Generation X* and *millennial* eras are tolerant as African American *baby boomers*. I don't believe that African American *Gen Xers and millennials* are as loyal to their employers as

African American *baby boomers* were to theirs, as evidenced by job hopping and short-term careers for which millennials are notorious. The majority of African American *baby boomers* I know, including myself, have retired from their jobs. I was employed with the Illinois Department of Human Services for 38 ½ years. My brother has been with his employer for 40 years, and he does not appear to be retiring soon. Whenever I ask him when he is going to retire, his response is always, "I don't know." Many of my African American friends have been on their jobs for over 20 years. I would be remiss not to mention that the workforce has changed significantly. Numerous American jobs have been sent overseas due to cheaper labor.

Why Do Americans Hate Americans?

CHAPTER 25

Some Suggestions Dealing with Racism in America

I do not profess to have all the answers to *racism*, but I do have some suggestions to help us to deal with it in our country. First, we need to better educate ourselves about other people who are different from us and whose culture, religion, beliefs, creed, sexual orientations, customs, music, language, clothes, ethnicity, etc. differ from ours. By doing this will enable us to learn about people in different perspectives. For instance, when we work together for a common cause, we stand to succeed. On the other hand, when we work separately and exclusively, we are divided and defeated. One of the amazing things I love about this country is its generosity, willingness and volunteerism when calamities afflict our country such as hurricanes, tornadoes, fires, floods, snowstorms, etc. Americans do an excellent job "pitching in" when it counts! No one cannot outgive us or outlove us. No one cannot outdo us when it comes to helping others who are in crises. Hurricane Katrina caused a great deal of chaos, destruction and confusion in our country, yet Americans responded *resiliently*. Of course, everything was not <u>perfect</u> or went smoothly or seamlessly, but thousands of people were helped and supported.

Secondly, we need to do a better job parenting to our children. Effective parenting is an issue in America. There are so many ways people tend to parent to their children. However, there is no right way or wrong way to parent. Parents tend to parent in the same way they were as children. Obviously, there are some pros and cons to that approach. As a parent myself, I wouldn't dare to parent to my daughters in the way I was parented by my parents. I will admit some of my parents' methods were unorthodox and perhaps a bit unusual. When my mom and I have this conversation about the methods she used to parent me and my siblings, she makes it clear that I would not be the "man" I am today. Of course, I cannot debate this. I know I have a lot of my mother's traits and personality characteristics. I am often teased about the tidiness and neatness of my house. My mother often says that my house is like a museum, meaning that no one appears to live in it. In response, I ask her "who was my trainer?" End of conversation! I will not go into details about the ways my two siblings and I were parented. But I would say that my siblings and I parent differently to our own children.

I believe the most difficult job God has given us on earth is to be parents. Children are a gift from God.

Unfortunately, not everyone has been blessed with biological children. Some people have adopted children, and have done a wonderful job of rearing, caring and loving them. I often hear adoptive parents refer to their adopted children as their own "children."

Children do not come into the world with manuals or instructions. However, I strongly believe all children need unconditional love, care and discipline. Discipline is teaching and training, not necessarily using corporal punishment. I know when some people hear the word discipline, they may think of harsh punishment. Of course, I am not talking about this type of discipline. Everyone needs discipline in his or her life. Without it, there will be nothing but chaos and confusion in our families. Children need structure. Structure enables children to learn character, respect, and teaches them conscience.

All children need unconditional love. Love is a very powerful tool to use when rearing children. When children know that you love them unconditionally, they will do anything and everything for you.

Personally, I believe in tough love. When children are given tough love, they will learn how to respect themselves and others. They will also learn how to respect life. I believe there are too many children and adults who do not respect life. This is one of the main reasons that we have such a skyrocketing homicide rate in America. No one wants to respect life. I believe if you cannot give life, you do not have a right to take life. This includes murder, wars, capital punishment and abortion. Life is a gift from God, and He is the only One who has a right to take life or give it.

No child asked to come into this world. Therefore, a child is entitled to proper care and sustenance. Children need proper care and a safe environment.

Research shows that children who are reared in safe environments tend to do well in school and are less likely to get involved in maladaptive behavior or juvenile delinquency. Moreover, children who eat their meals with their families tend to develop healthy relationships with their peers and are more sociable than those children who do not eat meals with their families. Families need to start eating their meals together on a regular basis. A regular basis would be at least six days per week. Besides, it is cheaper and healthier to have a home-cooked meal every day. If you do not know how to cook, learn how to cook.

Even though America is a very diverse country; however, there is so much division and discord among the races. It seems that every race and/or ethnic group is reluctant to venture out and interact with other Americans who are different from them. I often hear that diversity is good and is encouraged. However, diversity is only good if we are involved and engaged with each other. It serves no purpose to embrace diversity, if it does not encourage people to socialize, care, love and respect each other.

The word I often hear is "*tolerance*." Americans need to be tolerant of each other regardless of our race, religion, creed, ethnicity, sexual orientation, socioeconomic status (SES) and beliefs. Although I perceive *tolerance* as politically correct, I don't see it as reality. Reality is doing the right thing, and the right thing is treating everyone as equal and just. Period! It should not matter whether we can or cannot tolerate each other, but it matters most that we are consciously aware of our dislikes and prejudices toward other Americans. What I am saying here is that not everyone is not going to like everyone. Period.

We know this is a fact, and it is human behavior. However, we need to put ourselves in other people's shoes. Do the right thing and be fair about whatever you do to other people. It is human nature wanting to be liked, loved and treated with respect and dignity. Using these tenets in our dealings with each other would enable us to be cognizant and conscious of making better decisions under certain circumstances, when we interact or have contact with other Americans. I strongly believe the majority of Americans have a tendency to make preconceived notions about each other, based on their prior experiences. This is not the best way to live, or the best way to judge people. The best way to judge is to be in the moment, not thinking about what happened to you months or years ago or what you have heard from your circle of friends or family. Staying in the moment enhances your ability to make unbiased decisions and judgments. Making generalizations about people is not always appropriate.

In essence, we need to do a better job rearing our children. There is so much disappointment and anger toward our presidents, legislators, politicians and leaders. Americans are extremely displeased with the country's leadership. We really can't fault our leaders, because they, too, are Americans and are products of our families and homes. If we want better presidents, legislators, politicians and leaders to run our country, we need to do a better job training, molding, shaping and grooming our children so that they will develop character, loyalty and commitment.

America! We can do better, and we must do better!

Why Do Americans Hate Americans?

__Reflection__

CHAPTER 26

What Can Americans Do about Racism in America?

What can Americans do about *racism* in America? For starters, we can start with prevention, education, intervention, rehabilitation and justice. Each one of these deserves some elaboration. Preventing the social disease of *racism* is more than a notion. It needs to be a priority for all Americans. In order to eradicate *racism* in this country, we need to start valuing each other as human beings and provide the utmost respect, love, compassion for all. Perhaps this may seem easier said than done. However, I strongly believe this can be done through the following suggestions:

- Whenever you have the opportunity or occasion to encounter a person whose race, gender, creed, religion, sexual orientation, ethnicity, customs differ from yours, invite her or him out for a cup of coffee or tea. Try to develop a friendly or platonic relationship. (Remember you are not asking for a date. You just want to get to know the person as a human being). Period!

- Try to interact with another person who is completely different from you. For instance, if you are African American or Irish American, try to have a conversation about current events or your personal goals in life. Preferably, use this opportunity on your job or in your neighborhood. At the beginning of the conversation, make it light and general.

- While you are in the public, greet others by saying "hello." If possible, wish the person a wonderful day or evening. Sometimes a nod may be a good gesture, too. The intent here is just acknowledging people in your presence. In general, people like to be acknowledged and recognized.

- Do not make **generalizations** about people. Some people have a tendency to generalize and put certain people in categories for various reasons. Remember, people are not monolithic! This includes everyone from all walks of life and other countries!

- When you are in stores, restaurants or in public buildings, hold the door open for the person who is behind you. If there is a revolving door, offer the person to go first through the door. I have been doing this for years, and I am so amazed how reciprocal people have been with this small, friendly gesture.

- During the winter holiday seasons, some people are generally in the spirit of giving, caring, serving, etc. Why not make this a lifestyle? Let people know you care about them. There are many ways to help people besides giving money. Giving a few minutes of your time to listen is invaluable and priceless. You will be so surprised to find so many people who are in need of a listening ear. There are so many people who are in despair and distress.

- Some universities and high schools have made it mandatory for their students to volunteer their time to do community services. Volunteering in your community shows that you care and concerned about humankind. You can do mentorship or provide tutorial services to your local schools to students who need extra help in their subjects. Historically, Americans have been great volunteers.

- We all are spiritual beings. Our spirituality is often ignored and/or neglected. I am not necessarily talking about religion or Christianity. I am talking about being who you are and living out your purpose(s) in life. One of our purposes in life is to love. We can choose to love or hate. The choice is yours!

- Educating people about people is vital and essential. People need to know about each other's belief systems, customs, values, religion, music, foods, rituals, etc. As Americans, we should not be reluctant or hesitant to explore other Americans' lifestyles. America is a very diverse country, with people from social, economic and ethnic groups. *Education* starts at home. Parents need to educate their children and themselves about other Americans whose family structures differ from theirs. There is so much information on the Internet regarding the world, as well as in books and magazines. When you are educated about people who are different from yourself, you will have a better understanding and perspective about people in general. Because we are Americans and live in America does not preclude us from having an appreciation for people. Furthermore, just because you are American does not mean you know about America. Americans are not monolithic. For example, Puerto Rican Americans are different from Mexican Americans, and Mexican Americans are different from Cuban Americans. Irish Americans are different from Italian Americans and German Americans. Chinese

Americans are different from Japanese Americans and Japanese Americans are different from Korean Americans. Do you get the picture? Moreover, all African Americans are not the same or <u>monolithic</u>. Even in different parts of America, African Americans have different lifestyles, customs, belief systems and heritage. Hence, all African Americans are not the same or have the same lifestyle. I know the media tend to bend all African Americans in one group, but this is an unfortunate mistake, which causes misconceptions, stereotypes, prejudice and *racism*.

- *Intervention* may be necessary in some cases. Of course, there are people who are not interested in learning about other people or do not want to get along with certain Americans. Unfortunately, there will be Americans who will not behave themselves. Because of this, there will be times where *intervention* will be necessary, meaning that bad behavior needs to be addressed accordingly and people need to be held accountable for their inappropriate behavior. As I mentioned earlier in this book about the *hate crime* law, which I find repulsive and un-American, but it is necessary. When some Americans behave badly toward other Americans, there may be a time that the law enforcement may be necessary, especially when people have been bodily injured or treated unfairly.

It would be great, if we didn't need a *hate crime law* or any other laws to protect Americans against Americans. I have had numerous conversations with non-minorities about this matter. Many of them believe that it is unfair to have such a law. Furthermore, they do not believe society should be held responsible for what took place decades ago, during an era when they did not exist. Moreover, they believe that they should not be held accountable for the *racism* and *discrimination* that their <u>ancestors</u> caused in this country. To some extent, I somewhat agree. However, when I ask these individuals what they have done about *racism* and *discrimination* that have been perpetuating since then and currently, I often get a blank stare. What is so intriguing about the *hate crime law* is that it did not exist prior to the *Jim Crow laws* or the *Civil Rights Movement*. I would be completely naïve to believe that the *hate crime law* would had a chance to exist during these eras. However, what bothers me immensely is that our society has not made that much progress with racial relations and human rights for <u>all</u> <u>Americans</u>. Period! Apparently, <u>some</u> Americans have not done their part in making America a better country for <u>all Americans</u>. Ideally, it would be great if we did not need laws to protect Americans against Americans or the *hate crime law* in America. Until we can do a better a job as a country, we may need to continue to have laws to protect Americans against Americans.

- *Rehabilitation* may be necessary in some instances. *Rehabilitation* is often associated with prisoners who have been incarcerated and/or rehabilitated prior to being released from prison. I am using this term differently: In reference to ways to address *racism* in America, rehabilitating the minds of people would be a form of rehabilitation. For instance, restructuring and reshaping the way people think about each other would be a form of *rehabilitation*.

- *Justice* for all is something that is missing from our society. Of course, our Constitution stipulates this, but it is often not a reality in the day-to-day world. In light of this, Americans do not need laws, rules and regulations to govern their behavior, morals and character. Again, this is an issue about treating people the same way you want to be treated. In essence, putting yourself in another person's shoes would be ideal.

When I was a forensic psychologist, there was immense emphasis placed on evidence-based practice. What this means is that the practice of psychology should be based on scientific evidence of research and methodology related to the delivery of mental health services provided to patients who were experiencing mental illness or mental disorders.

Of course, there are different standards and/or criteria of evidence-based practice in the health care profession. Each profession has its own scientific criteria of evidence-based practice. What is my point?

Since I suggested that *racism* is a social disease, it would need its own evidence-based practice. However, I have not used any scientific research to support my standards of evidence-based practice. In spite of this, I am providing my own evidence-based practice related to *racism* in America. 1.). Treating *racism* holistically, not in fragments. 2.). Adapting effective methods and ways to eradicate *racism* in America. 3.). Holding Americans accountable for the future of this country. 4.). Preparing future generations to continue to combat *racism*. 5.).Training multicultural professionals to provide education and prevention of *racism*. 6.). Working collectively and collaboratively as Americans. 7.). Assuring action plans take precedence over laws, policies and legislations. 8.). Redefining *multiculturism* as it relates to *racism*. 9.). Educating Americans about *racism*, as well as working toward common goals to eradicate it. 10.). Americanizing Americans to become

Americans. 11.). Redefining America for the future.

Why Do Americans Hate Americans?

Reflection

_____

_____

_____

_____

_____

_____

_____

_____

_____

_____

_____

_____

_____

_____

CHAPTER 27

I Love America

In spite of its imperfections, fallibilities, shortcomings and problems, I love my country!! America is the best country to live. It is the richest and most resourceful country on earth. It seems that everyone wants to come and live in America. I have met so many people abroad who want to live in this country. When Americans are at peace and civil, there are no other people on earth who can outgive us or outlove us! I have some good experiences and not-so-good experiences with Americans (including African Americans) whose religion, custom, beliefs, gender, sexual orientation, and socioeconomic status (SES) differ from mine. I know we are dealing with some challenging and unprecedented times with the pandemic, unrest and *racism*, but I strongly believe and hope that America will overcome these calamities, infirmities and crises, with the help of God! God is the only One who can get us through these extraordinary difficult and hard times. We experienced His Omnipotence during the Great Depression. We experienced His Omnipotence during the aftermath of 9/11. In addition, we will experience His Omnipotence in the aftermath of 2020. As long as we are living, there is hope. With hope, we can do anything, with the help of God! I know there are many people who are angry with God, and I know some people removed Him from their lives, as evidenced by the absence of God in our schools, public facilities, jobs, government, courts and homes. We can also put Him back in our schools, public facilities, jobs, government, courthouses and homes, where He belongs!

America was built on the foundation of God (In God We Trust). These are words on our currencies, and they used to be posted on the walls in our courts, municipality and government buildings.

Why Do Americans Hate Americans?

Reflection

_____

_____

_____

_____

_____

_____

_____

_____

_____

_____

_____

_____

_____

_____

_____

Author's Biography

Dr. Daniel Williams Jr. has over 26 years of clinical experience in mental health. He has worked in forensic psychology, treating adult patients who were unfit to stand trial. He also treated emotionally disturbed children and adolescents in an inpatient psychiatric facility. Dr. Williams was a faculty member for 10 years at the University of Phoenix. While a faculty member, he taught graduate and undergraduate psychology courses. He also taught graduate psychology courses at Buena Vista University in Storm Lake, Iowa. Dr. Williams has a doctorate degree in clinical psychology from the Illinois School of Professional Psychology (ISPP) in Rolling Meadows, Illinois; he earned his master's degree in clinical psychology from ISPP; he has a master's degree in social work from the University of Illinois at Chicago, and a B.A. from George Williams College in Downers Grove, Illinois. Moreover, he is an ordained minister and a former professional baseball player with the Pittsburgh Pirates Organization. He is a member of the American Psychological Association (APA), and a member of the Screen Actors Guild (SAG). Dr. Williams can be contacted at one of the following social media: drdanielwilliamsjr@att.net   http://www.focusonme.us. Twitter@drfocusOnme.com

Facebook@FOCUSonMe.com.